THE WONKY SPATULA

COOK HEALTHY, LIVE HAPPY

NICOLA HALLORAN

ORPEN PRESS

Published by
Orpen Press
Upper Floor, Unit B3
Hume Centre, Hume Avenue
Park West Industrial Estate
Dublin 12
Ireland

email: info@orpenpress.com
www.orpenpress.com

ISBN 978-1-78605-104-2

Printed by Gutenberg Press Ltd Malta

ags, if you were here we'd need
o get you some new buttons for
our shirt because I know you
ould be bursting with pride.
Beep Beep, Nic xo

THANK YOU, THANK YOU, THANK YOU!

Firstly, the biggest thank you of all has got to be to my super-star parents, Hazel and Noel, who have stuck with me throughout this journey and put up with their kitchen being turned into a test kitchen and photography studio for more weekends than I care to remember! From being taste-testers, to kitchen porters, holding up bedsheets to yield the best light – they really have been there through it all.

It also doesn't just extent to just the last couple of months; they have supported me from the very beginning of the Wonky Spatula journey, which is six years in the making, and for that I am eternally grateful.

To my amazing team of proof-readers (and occasional taste-testers): Keith, Helen, Lauren and David – thank you for giving up large chunks of your Easter weekend to take on the mammoth task of sense-checking, proof-reading and putting up with the madness!

Eileen, words cannot describe how amazing it was to meet someone who got exactly what I was trying to do and helped me drive it through into a reality. Thank you to you and the whole team at Orpen for getting behind me and my wonky spatula!

Thank you to Sarah for visualising my dream layout and helping me make it a reality and to Evan for capturing those all-important pictures that I could not.

The final thank you? Well that has to be to you, the reader. Thank you for taking the time to read my book. It means more than I could possibly squeeze into a few lines. From those of you who have been long-standing followers of the Wonky Spatula right through to those who are meeting me (in print(!)) for the first time, thank you from the bottom of my heart and I hope that you find some recipes you love.

CONTENTS

INTRODUCTION

There is no such thing as a bad cook

INTRODUCTION –
THE WONKY SPATULA

You may not know this but The Wonky Spatula originally started out back in 2014 as a simple list of healthy foods. From there it grew, alongside my mission to show people the tasty way to be healthy.

Healthy by no means has to be boring. In fact, with the right knowledge of how to prepare different ingredients you can make some of the best food you've ever eaten at home, in the comfort of your own kitchen.

Before I started this journey I had pretty limited experience when it came to cooking. Over time I got comfortable with both my kitchen and Google, preparing all of my own meals from scratch for the first time ever. As I learned new techniques and tried out new flavours, I grew more confident and adventurous. Food became far more than just functional, taking on a new role in my life as I uncovered a passion I never knew existed.

As you read through all of the recipes in this book, you'll see a common theme emerge – family meals – with a heavy influence on my style in the kitchen coming from my parents. I guess having seen things happen in the kitchen in my peripheral vision over the years something must have rubbed off on me. But if food and cooking hasn't been something that has played a part in the background of your life please don't be put off.

What I want you to take from this book is that there is no such thing as someone who cannot cook; with the right tools and guidance we all have it in us. If there's ever a technique or ingredient that you're unsure of, don't let that stop you. Take a couple of minutes, find out what it is and give it a try – what's the worst that can happen, you might not like it? Or you could discover something that you absolutely adore and have been missing out on.

Cook healthy, live happy!

Nicola x

 thewonkyspatula.com

    @thewonkyspatula

Healthy habits are formed by doing the things you love

IS THIS BOOK FOR YOU?

This book is for you if …

You want to find your feet in the kitchen, but you don't know where to start.

You've tried to learn how to cook in the past, but you just couldn't get your head around it.

You're bored by the thoughts of chicken and broccoli 24/7.

You're busy, stressed and short on time and need a no-BS approach to cooking.

You struggle to get motivated to cook healthy food.

You find weekly food planning overwhelming.

You're overwhelmed by all the mixed messages out there when it comes to what healthy food is.

You want to make lasting healthy changes to your lifestyle.

You want to find an approach to food and fitness that is sustainable and fits into your demanding day-to-day life.

*None of the above sound like you? Keep reading anyway. You never know what you'll find ☺

KEY SYMBOLS USED IN THE BOOK

 Easy   Medium   Hard

 Dairy Free   Gluten Free   Vegan   Paleo   30 min (or less)

A healthy outside starts from the inside

WHAT IS HEALTHY EATING?

WHAT DOES HEALTHY EATING MEAN?

At the beginning of my health food journey I went strict paleo and eliminated certain food groups for no particular reason other than I was following a diet that recommended doing so. I stuck to this style of eating for a little over two years; I felt amazing and delighted in telling people all about it, encouraging them to do the same. Then along came the Instagram craze of oats, zoats/proats … suddenly I could see so many people on my feed enjoying these amazing-looking bowls which for the first time ever gave me severe food envy, as the way I was eating did not allow oats to be included.

I sat back one afternoon and thought to myself – is this the way I can see myself eating for the rest of my life? For the longest time I would have told you absolutely and couldn't imagine a time when this wasn't the case. But, slowly I began to see that this wasn't sustainable for me in the long run. I realised that I was missing out on certain things as a result. Yes I could continue on, but in reality I would probably regret it in years to come.

Conscious of just throwing out the 'rule book' that I had followed so rigidity for so long, I started slowly. Trying out 'new' foods. Oats, chickpeas, lentils, peanut butter … the odd piece of white chocolate here and there. After a couple of months I didn't know myself. I had a new-found flexibility. I could eat out without being 'that' person; I had no problem trying the odd thing that would be considered 'bad' for you. As a result my relationship with food and my loved ones completely changed and I delighted in going out to try new things no longer bound by a series of rules that had kept me from discovering amazing foods and flavours.

Alongside the food side of things, I also diversified my exercise style and found new loves there too. After a few months of implementing a series of small incremental changes it suddenly dawned on me: I had struck a perfect balance in all aspects of my life. With that came an amazing sense of freedom; I could decide what I wanted to say yes to, there were no longer any rules in place when it came to my version of what was healthy. And dare I say it, I became even more of a foodie as a result.

Of course I still hold the same principles when it comes to eating – fresh, unprocessed, seasonal food. Buying Irish and supporting Irish food businesses is something I am very passionate about.

> **What being healthy is, is completely unique to you**

But the main piece of knowledge I came away with was that what being healthy is, is completely unique to you. No two people's plates will ever be identical, nor should they be – after all do any two bodies look the same? No! So, come on board and let me help you unlock the secrets to a plate that's full of freedom to enjoy the things you love.

Gone are the days of restrictive diets, bland food choices, deprivation and feeling like a zombie. To me, diets are unsustainable short-term fixes. Rather my focus is on making small incremental changes that are sustainable within your life and don't leave you feeling as if you are missing out.

Food is there to be savoured and enjoyed; I want to give you the tools that help you to enjoy all of the things you love, leaving you feeling energised, healthy and ready to take on anything that life throws at you. How do you achieve this? 'Balance!' But is there any sense to it or is it just for Instagram?

Make small incremental changes that are sustainable

Let me demystify the mystical concept of balance – many of us have heard this term being thrown around all over social media but do we really know what it means? There is no one true meaning or formula as everyone's balance is different and comes in many forms.

And that's why I actually have a bit of time for balance. It's a concept that is unique to each person, much like our bodies are unique and in turn our plates should be unique too.

For me, balance centres around fuelling my body to the best of my ability, making informed food choices on a daily basis while allowing flexibility when it comes to social occasions with family, friends and loved ones. In tandem with this, carving out time to move on a daily basis – whether it's a long walk, heading to the gym or giving it my all at a boxing class.

When it comes to balance, nutrition is paramount; once you have nailed this down with an approach where you feel that you could happily eat the way you are currently eating for the rest of your life, all other elements will simply fall into place as a knock-on effect.

Eating fresh, unprocessed, seasonal food plays a huge part in finding your balance. Obviously in an ideal world we would all just eat our favourite foods 24/7 with no consequences; however, it's highly doubtful that everyone's favourite meals have a good balance of carbohydrates, protein and fat to keep our bodies functioning to the best of their abilities.

Now don't get me wrong, I'm by no means telling you to put down that piece of pizza/chocolate/ whatever it may be – I'm simply going to give you the tools to enjoy a healthy lifestyle that allows for these types of things while also fuelling your body with all the key nutrients it needs and deserves.

You should be excited about the meals you are eating on a daily basis; if you are not enjoying your food there's something wrong with your approach. It could be that you've lost your mojo a bit when it comes to trying new things – if so then you've come to the right place. The recipes in this book are easy to follow and pack a serious punch in the flavour department.

I want to help you navigate through *real life*, with real-life recipes using real ingredients you can get in your local supermarket.

WHAT IS FOOD?

Yes, food is fuel for our bodies but it is also there to be savoured and enjoyed; it is so much more than just a functional transaction. That being said, we do need to ensure that we are giving our bodies all of the nutrients they need in order to thrive.

We quite literally are what we eat; every piece of food that we ingest is broken down in our bodies and used to help us to live, breathe and grow.

What we eat affects not only how we look and feel but also how we function. In order to feel healthy, energised and have our bodies performing at their best we need to fill them with nourishing, wholesome foods – packed full of colour and flavour. You don't need to eat chicken and broccoli 24/7 to achieve this either. This book is packed full of delicious food that will make you feel amazing. So let's get down to it.

Our bodies need nutrients in order to function and these are broken down into macro and micro nutrients. Don't worry, I'm not going to get too technical or have you counting every calorie under the sun. It's just important to explain these principles and their role in creating healthy eating habits.

Macronutrients are the essential nutrients we need to consume in large quantities to metabolise for energy. They're broken down into three categories: proteins, fats and carbohydrates. Micronutrients are just as essential but are required in smaller amounts; they include all of the key vitamins and minerals your body needs to function. A balanced plate has a good spread across each of the macronutrients and also features micronutrients.

For me a balanced plate is one-quarter filled with protein (such as meat, fish, chicken, tofu), one-quarter filled with carbohydrates (like potatoes, pasta, rice, quinoa) and one-half filled with colourful vegetables (non-starchy colourful veggies like kale, cabbage, tomatoes, courgette, and so on). Fats are then throughout the plate in the form of the cooking oil, a scattering of nuts or some avocado.

It's important to embrace your plate – none of these food groups should be feared or shied away from; they are there to help you build the most delicious meals possible and have your body functioning at its very best.

Embrace your plate

FIVE THINGS YOU NEED TO KNOW ABOUT HOW TO EAT

Eating is something we all learn how to do at such a young age. Yes, you've grown up eating food your entire life. But chances are you were never taught how to truly eat properly. To get the full benefit from your nutrition, here's five quick tips you can use to get the most out of your food.

IT TAKES AT LEAST 20 MINUTES TO FEEL FULL

Bear this in mind when you get to the end of a meal and don't quite feel satisfied. You should only eat until you are comfortably full, not stuffed. Eating slowly can greatly aid this, giving time for your brain to register exactly what is going on and tell your body to stop eating before you're overfull.

We've all been there. Eating until you are stuffed like a turkey at Christmas is not fun so relax and take your time; you'll enjoy your food all the more for it. And if you do find yourself stuffed to the brim, head out for a light walk rather than retreat to the couch – you'll feel all the better for it, trust me.

CHEW YOUR FOOD THOROUGHLY

You can massively improve your digestion by chewing your food correctly. It helps to break food down into smaller pieces and mix saliva into them to start the breakdown process sooner.

CHEW LIQUID FOODS

This is one you've probably never even thought about but even liquids need to have saliva mixed into them in order to break down properly in our stomach. Give things like smoothies a little chew or a swish around your mouth; this mixes the important enzymes in your saliva into them, again kick-starting the digestion process.

EAT MINDFULLY

This is definitely something we all struggle with – particularly if you come home ravenous after a busy day. Rather than inhaling food on the go, something we're all guilty of, try to take a moment to bring your awareness back to what you are eating. Put your phone down, turn off the TV and think about what you're eating. What does it smell like? What does it taste like?

EAT ENOUGH CALORIES TO FUEL YOUR BODY

As much as I am in no way suggesting you start counting calories, it is important to note that they do count. Your breakdown of calories in versus calories out will equate to whether you gain, lose or maintain weight.

We can often overestimate how many calories we burn and also totally underestimate the amount we consume. So bear this in mind when choosing your foods and strike a volume balance that works for you and your body.

Top tips for planning your week on a plate:

- ✓ Breakfast should always come in the form of cupboard staples; there's no need to complicate it and it's always a good plan to change it up regularly.
- ✓ Plan your dinners ahead of your lunches; that way you can incorporate leftovers or cook additional bits and pieces at the same time.
- ✓ Build out your lunchbox with veggies and grains, cook smart in the evenings and prepare it at the same time as your dinner (the Wonky Salad on page 75 is a great tool to help with this).
- ✓ Reduce food waste as much as possible by doing a thorough scan of your fridge/freezer and cupboards before hitting the shops.
- ✓ Always make a list when you head out for groceries, and stick to it.

HOW TO NAVIGATE THE WORKING WEEK

A busy work life can take its toll on your body, both physically and mentally. Then pair that with trying to stay on track with healthy eating, which isn't always easy, especially when there seems to always be a birthday cake, pastries or even sausage rolls doing the rounds.

Obviously I'm not expecting or suggesting that you say no to absolutely everything as the main thing we're striving for is a healthy relationship with food, and if a pastry every now and then is something you enjoy then who am I to step in your way? Rather than preach that X or Y is bad, I want to give you the tools to put your best foot forward when it comes to making informed decisions.

There are a lot of things that can derail your healthy intentions at work, whether it is having to stay late, a last-minute lunch – you name it I've heard it, and have also experienced it. On top of that, most people are also restricted in terms of facilities/access to healthy food nearby, which can make it even more difficult. So how do you overcome this and establish healthy habits at work?

PREP FOR THE WEEK AHEAD

When it comes to healthy eating, preparation is the key to success. Planning and preparing your meals ahead of time will make healthy choices a no-brainer. Instead of running to the local deli, you'll have a home-cooked feast on hand that can be heated up faster than you can walk to the shop. A bigger bonus is that in the long run, you will save yourself some extra money, win–win.

GET ACTIVE AS OFTEN AS POSSIBLE

Use your lunch break to squeeze in a walk; especially if you spend the majority of your day sitting, getting up and leaving your desk allows you to stretch the legs and loosen up those hip flexors.

TAKE YOUR LUNCH HOUR

Eating while you work means that you are multi-tasking. Your attention isn't on your work, and it is certainly not on the food that you are most likely inhaling. In order to be a healthy eater, you need to pay attention to what you are eating. You will enjoy your food more. You will ingest less of it. And, as a result, you should see the health benefits as well.

PLOT IN A WORKOUT

Often times if you work in a sedentary job, sitting and concentrating for eight hours a day can leave you exhausted and the last thing you want to do is exercise. However, getting out and being active for even 30 minutes each evening will do you the world of good, increasing your energy levels and boosting your mood.

For me working out after a busy day is the best de-stressor on the planet – you're forced to leave your thoughts at the door and concentrate on keeping one foot in front of the other. Group environments are my personal preference for midweek workouts; surround yourself with likeminded people and enjoy the process.

PLAN SOMETHING NICE FOR YOUR EVENING

It's super important to switch off at the end of the day, whether you curl up on the couch with a good book, spend some time with friends or try something new out in the kitchen; downtime is the key to a healthy working week.

A weekend well spent sets you up for a great week ahead

MAKE THE MOST OF YOUR WEEKENDS

A weekend well spent sets you up for a great week ahead. Weekends are there to be savoured and enjoyed – much like food. However, you don't want to go totally overboard – as with everything there's a sweet spot when it comes to how to set yourself up for success both during and after.

START WITH A GOOD NIGHT'S SLEEP

Just because you don't have to be up early doesn't mean you should throw your usual sleep habits out the window. It's super important that you are getting enough quality sleep throughout the week, not just Monday to Friday.

Sleep plays such an important role on your physical health. You might be surprised to learn that poor sleep can be linked to weighing more as good sleepers tend to consume fewer calories. Good quality sleep also boosts your mood, and increases your productivity and your immune system.

BEGIN YOUR DAY WITH BREAKFAST

If you sleep later than usual on the weekends make sure you get up a couple of hours before lunch and have something small to get your metabolism going.

MOVE YOUR BODY

Don't turn into a couch potato, as much as you might be tempted to retreat after a busy week – be sure to get out for some fresh air. Head to the gym, go for a long walk or cycle, try out a class you wouldn't have time for during the week.

Whatever your preference, getting out and getting active is a great way to boost your mood.

DON'T SKIP MEALS

We've all been there – you're heading out for a big dinner so you decide to skimp on the rest of your meals for the day in order to 'make room' or 'save up' for it. It's so important that you still eat as normal during the day; if you starve yourself you'll end up eating more than you would normally and feeling overly full/regretting it the next day rather than looking back on a fabulous meal.

WATCH THE ALCOHOL

As much as I love the odd tipple (who doesn't?), alcohol has absolutely no nutritional benefit. Between Friday night drinks after work, cocktails with the girls on Saturday followed by bottomless brunch or a few glasses of red with dinner on Sunday, what you might only see as a couple of glasses here and there really adds up.

Just because alcohol has no nutritional benefits doesn't mean that it isn't loaded with calories so make smart choices; clear liquids and low-calorie mixers are the way to go! (Gin and slim ... need I say anymore ☺) Be mindful of the quantity you are consuming – swap one or two alcoholic drinks with non-alcoholic ones; no one will be any the wiser and trust me, you'll be thanking me when you wake up hangover-free.

Most importantly, say yes to things and do whatever makes you happy – the weekends are there to be enjoyed whatever way you see fit.

KEY COOKING TECHNIQUES AND PANTRY

This section is packed full of key cooking techniques, acting as a quick and easy how-to guide from poaching eggs, preparing stocks, making your own nut butters and much, much more.

It is a selection of things that I wish I had had to hand when starting off in the kitchen. I hope you find this section useful and if you have any questions feel free to drop me a message on Instagram, Facebook or Twitter @thewonkyspatula – happy cooking!

STORING FOOD

FIRST UP, LET'S CHAT ABOUT THE FRIDGE

There are a few simple rules to live by when it comes to using your fridge in the best possible way. First and foremost, keep raw and cooked foods separately. Place cooked and ready-to-eat items towards the top, and keep raw food on the bottom/lower shelves if possible. The idea here is to reduce cross-contamination between cooked and raw food.

Meat is something that you need to be pretty vigilant with. Use within its sell-by date and ensure that you keep it in sealed airtight containers. When I go to my local butchers I tend to unpack everything from the bags they come in and place in Tupperware.

Believe it or not, food can sometimes freeze in your fridge so make sure that you keep salads and herbs away from the back of the fridge and do not let them touch the back wall – the temperature at the back is colder and these types of foods could freeze.

Dairy should be kept in the middle of your fridge but things like butter and soft cheeses don't need to be in the coldest part of the fridge so I find that the door shelves are best for this. Similarly with eggs – if you like to keep them in the fridge the door is best.

Open jars – mustard, pesto, curry paste, etc. – should be kept in the fridge. It's really important here that you regularly check this section as often there is a limit on how long an item can be open before it goes out of date. Always check this before you reuse something that's been open for a while.

When it comes to defrosting something the best place to do this is in the fridge; clear a space at the bottom of the fridge and leave the item there, preferably overnight, to defrost. I tend to take my meat out for the next day before I go to bed; then when you come home in the evening it's ready to go. Obviously larger items like whole chickens take longer to defrost so take this into consideration when planning your meals.

The fridge temperature is something that is so important. You should be aiming to keep your fridge at the same temperature all of the time, so don't leave the door open while you ponder what you're going to make for dinner and always avoid putting hot food in the fridge as it causes the overall temperature to rise. Leave cooked food out to cool for a couple of hours (90 minutes is optimum) and then place in the fridge.

Just like everything in the kitchen, cleanliness is paramount. It may be the last thing that crosses your mind but it's super important to regularly clean out the inside of your fridge. Alongside this, it's a good idea to thaw it out every so often too in order to avoid a build-up of ice.

So, to recap –

Upper shelves	Pre-cooked items like deli meats, leftovers, etc.
Lower/middle shelves	Dairy – milks, cheese, yogurt, etc.
Bottom shelf	Raw meat and fish
Drawers	Vegetables that need to be kept in the fridge and herbs
Door	Condiments (mustard, mint sauce, curry paste, pesto, etc.), juices, butter and eggs

GET FRIENDLY WITH YOUR FREEZER

I cannot stress what a difference using your freezer wisely makes to your day-to-day life.

There's so much more to your freezer than just storing typical freezer items – ice, ice-cream, frozen peas, etc. It is the perfect kitchen partner to help you prepare meals in advance, preserve food that otherwise would go to waste and stay on top of your cooking. Use it as your secret weapon by stocking it up on days when you have more time so that when you need it most those essential items are there.

I literally freeze everything – most commonly found items in mine outside of the 'norm' are: chopped veggies that would have otherwise gone to waste (peppers, sweet potato, etc.), ginger, lemon juice, stock, herbs and fruit (I'm particularly fond of freezing lemon and lime wedges to use in place of ice-cubes!).

Use the space wisely. My mum is the maestro when it comes to getting the most out of the space in your freezer so I've learned from the best. A top tip for making the most of the space is to use freezer bags; this allows you to lay things on top of each other.

Rotation of food is paramount. Just because you have something in the freezer doesn't mean it will last forever. Date things as you put them into the freezer and operate on a first in, first out approach.

- *Avoid waste by freezing unused food before it goes out of date.* This applies to both prepared food and fresh fruit/veg and meat. You can freeze anything that hasn't already been frozen. So have a look at your labels and if something can be frozen pop it in.
- *Freeze chopped vegetables and herbs.* I am always harping on about this one. Pre-chopping and then freezing vegetables and herbs is a great way to cut down on time in the kitchen and it's also a great way to avoid food waste if they wouldn't have been eaten otherwise.

  For veggies, give them a wash and chop them up ready to go when you need them. Roughly chop herbs and pop them into an ice cube tray and pour over some olive oil to cover before placing in your freezer. Alternatively, you can mix them into soft butter perfect for melting into some hasselback potatoes at a later stage.

Item	How long you can freeze it for
White fish	6–8 months
Oily fish	3–4 months
Shellfish	2–3 months
Beef	4–6 months
Lamb	4–6 months
Pork	4–6 months
Sliced bacon	2–3 months
Cured meat	2–3 months
Ham/bacon joints	3–4 months
Chicken/turkey	4–6 months
Duck	4–6 months
Blanched vegetables	10–12 months
Unblanched vegetables	3–4 months
Vegetable/fruit purées	6–8 months
Fresh fruit	6–8 months
Fruit juice	4–6 months
Soups and sauces	3 months
Stocks	6 months
Prepared meals	4–6 months
Cakes	4–6 months
Bread	4–6 months
Butter	4–6 months
Ice-cream	3–4 months

- *Freeze your stock.* If you're lucky enough to have leftover chicken carcass from a roast make up a batch of stock and freeze it. The same applies to all types of stock – veg, beef, fish, you name it.

- *Freeze future dinners.* Batch cooking and freezing the leftovers in portions is a great way to help out your future self! I always freeze a couple of portions of spag bol/chilli con carne to have in the freezer for days when I need a quick and easy meal. The key here is to portion it out and freeze in singles or doubles so that you don't end up with any waste.

- *Freeze and refreeze.* We've discussed how things can go past their use-by date in the freezer but what happens if you have something in there that's about to go to past the point of no return but you have no occasion to use it? What do you do? Well, let me let you in on the best-kept secret of all – you can refreeze items **IF** you change their state. For example, you have a raw chicken in your freezer, it's been in there for six months so you need to use it up but you know that you won't be able to eat the whole thing by yourself. Take it out of the freezer, defrost it and cook it (I recommend my harissa chicken on page 119); the next day freeze your leftovers and it will keep for 4–6 more months. This is a really good opportunity for you to portion out the chicken at this stage so that you can take it out as/when you need it.

Some vegetables and fruit need to be stored in the fridge and others are best stored at room temperature or in a cool dry place. But how do you decide what you put, where and when?

Item	Where do you keep it	How long does it keep for
Potatoes	Cool room	2+ weeks
Onions	Cool room	1–2 months
Garlic	Cool room	3–4 weeks
Ginger	Cool room	3–4 weeks
Tomatoes	Room temperature	1–5 days
Avocados*	Room temperature	5 days
Spring Onions	Room temperature (in water)	1 week
Asparagus	Fridge	5 days
Broccoli	Fridge	3–5 days
Brussels Sprouts	Fridge	3–5 days
Cabbage	Fridge	1 week
Carrots	Fridge	3–4 weeks
Cauliflower	Fridge	1 week
Celery	Fridge	1–2 weeks
Cucumber	Fridge	1 week
Courgette	Fridge	5 days
Chillies	Fridge	5 days
Lettuce	Fridge	1 week
Mushrooms	Fridge	1 week
Parsnips	Fridge	3–4 weeks
Peppers	Fridge	1–2 weeks
Baby Potatoes	Fridge	1 week
Spinach	Fridge	3–5 days

* Keep avocados in your fruit bowl next to bananas to allow them to ripen – once ripe use within 1 day or place in the fridge for 2–3 days to preserve/stop ripening further.

Throughout my recipes you will see that in the ingredients section I call for different vegetables to be prepared in different ways.

The below illustrates exactly what I mean by each term.

Sliced

Diced / Cubed

Thin Strips

Minced

HOW TO EAT SEASONALLY

BENEFITS OF EATING IN SEASON

I am a major advocate of eating seasonal produce; local fruit and vegetables that are in season taste sensational!

- Better flavour – vegetables that are in season have a much better flavour as they are picked when they are fully ripe, so they truly taste amazing.
- Better nutrition – when produce is picked before its ripe, the nutrients don't fully develop in the flesh of the fruit/veg. Plants need the sun to grow, and picking them before they're ripe cuts off the nutrient availability.
- Environmentally friendly – less miles for your food to travel before it gets to your plate.
- Cost effective – seasonal produce tends to be slightly cheaper and also supports the local community.
- Finally, when you eat seasonally you are guaranteed to consume a wider variety of food.

The below chart is the perfect guide to follow when it comes to nailing seasonal eating – you can pick a new veggie to try out every month. Please note that this guide is specific to Ireland. Seasonality varies from country to country so be sure to check out what's in season wherever you are!

Legend: In season | Coming in or out of season | From storage

Vegetables	Jan	Feb	Mar	Apr	May	Jun	Jul	Aug	Sep	Oct	Nov	Dec
Asparagus				▨	▨	▨	▨					
Aubergines									▨			
Beetroot	▨	▨	▨	▨	▨	▨	▨	▨	▨	▨	▨	
Broad Beans					▨	▨	▨	▨	▨			
Broccoli (green)					▨	▨	▨	▨	▨	▨	▨	▨
Broccoli (purple sprouting)	▨	▨	▨	▨							▨	▨
Brussels Sprouts	▨	▨	▨						▨	▨	▨	▨
Cabbage	▨	▨	▨	▨	▨	▨	▨	▨	▨	▨	▨	▨
Carrots	▨	▨	▨		▨		▨	▨	▨	▨	▨	▨
Cauliflower	▨	▨	▨	▨	▨	▨	▨	▨	▨	▨	▨	▨
Celeriac	▨	▨	▨	▨					▨	▨	▨	▨
French Beans						▨	▨	▨	▨	▨		
Kale	▨	▨	▨	▨				▨	▨	▨	▨	▨
Leeks	▨	▨	▨	▨					▨	▨	▨	▨
Mangetout						▨	▨	▨	▨	▨		
Marrows							▨	▨	▨	▨	▨	
Mushrooms	▨	▨	▨	▨	▨	▨	▨	▨	▨	▨	▨	▨
Onions	▨	▨	▨	▨	▨	▨		▨	▨	▨	▨	▨
Pak Choi	▨			▨	▨	▨	▨	▨	▨	▨	▨	▨
Parsnips	▨	▨	▨	▨					▨	▨	▨	▨
Peas						▨	▨	▨	▨	▨		
Potatoes (main crop)	▨	▨	▨	▨	▨	▨	▨	▨	▨	▨	▨	▨
Potatoes (new season)					▨	▨	▨	▨				
Rhubarb			▨	▨	▨	▨			▨	▨		
Runner Beans						▨	▨	▨	▨	▨		
Shallots					▨				▨			
Spinach				▨	▨	▨	▨	▨	▨	▨	▨	
Swedes	▨	▨	▨	▨	▨	▨			▨	▨	▨	▨
Turnips	▨	▨	▨	▨	▨							

	In season		Coming in or out of season		From storage	

Legend: ■ In season ◧ Coming in or out of season ░ From storage

Fruit	Jan	Feb	Mar	Apr	May	Jun	Jul	Aug	Sep	Oct	Nov	Dec
Apples: Cooking	░	░	░	░	░	░	░	░	■	■	■	░
Apples: Eating	░	░	░	░	░			■		░	░	░
Blackberries						◧	■	■	■			
Blackcurrants						◧	■					
Blueberries							◧	■	■			
Gooseberries					◧	■	■					
Loganberries						■	■	■				
Raspberries						◧	■	■	■	■	■	
Strawberries				◧	■	■	■	■	■	■		
Tayberries							■					

Salads	Jan	Feb	Mar	Apr	May	Jun	Jul	Aug	Sep	Oct	Nov	Dec
Celery						■	■	■	■	■	■	■
Courgettes					■	■	■	■	■	■		
Cucumbers				◧	■	■	■	■	■	■		
Lettuce (iceberg)					◧	■	■	■	■	■		
Lettuce (lollo rosso)						■	■	■	■	■		
Lettuce (red oakleaf)						■	■	■	■	■		
Lettuce (round)	◧	◧				■	■	■	■	■		
Peppers				◧	■	■	■	■	■	■	■	
Radish				◧	■	■	■	■	■	■	■	
Scallions				◧	■	■	■	■	■	■	■	
Tomatoes					◧	■	■	■	■	■	■	

Herbs	Jan	Feb	Mar	Apr	May	Jun	Jul	Aug	Sep	Oct	Nov	Dec
Basil				◧	■	■	■	■	■	■	■	■
Chives					◧	■	■	■	■	■	■	■
Coriander					◧	■	■	■	■	■	◧	
Dill					◧	■	■	■	■	■	■	
Fennel						◧	■	■	■	■	■	
Mint			◧	■	■	■	■	■	■	■	■	◧
Parsley	◧			◧	■	■	■	■	■	■	■	■
Sage	◧			■	■	■	■	■	■	■	■	■
Thyme	◧			■	■	■	■	■	■	■	■	■

HOW TO COOK ...

EGGS

Hen's eggs are graded in four sizes: small, medium, large and very large. This relates both to their size and weight: small eggs are 53g and under; medium, 53–63g; large, 63–73g; and very large 73g and above. The size of eggs does not affect their quality but it does affect their price. When buying your eggs there are a couple of things to bear in mind:

- The eggshell should be clean, well-shaped and slightly tough.

- When eggs are broken there should be a high proportion of thick white to thin and the yolk should be firm, round and of an even colour.

- Always open the box of eggs when you are in the supermarket before adding them to your basket – check that they are clean, all look similar and, most importantly, that none are cracked. Always discard cracked eggs.

- Once you get them home, store in a cool dry place.

There are so many amazing different ways you can cook eggs – fried, scrambled, poached, boiled ... you name it – omelettes!

HOW TO BOIL AN EGG

1. Place the eggs in cold water and bring to the boil.

2. Once the water has come to the boil, reduce the heat and simmer.

3. The length of time you simmer for will depend on how you would like them cooked:

   - Soft: simmer for 2–2.5 minutes

   - Medium: simmer for 4–5 minutes

   - Hard: simmer for 8–10 minutes

4. Remove from the water and serve straight away in an egg cup.

HOW TO FRY AN EGG

1. Heat some oil/fat in a frying pan.

2. Add the eggs and cook gently until lightly set and serve.

HOW TO POACH AN EGG

1. Bring a large pot of water to the boil.

2. Reduce the heat to a gentle boil and add 1–2 tbsp of apple cider/white wine/malt vinegar.

3. Carefully break the eggs and place into the pot one by one.

4. Swirl the water with a slotted spoon and allow the eggs to cook for 3–3.5 minutes, until lightly set.

5. Remove carefully with a slotted spoon, serve and enjoy.

MEAT

First and foremost when it comes to meat, storing it correctly is essential – head to pages 19–22 to check out how to correctly store it in your fridge/freezer.

So you're more than likely aware that all raw meats can carry bacteria. Whole cuts of red meat, like a steak, only carry bacteria on the outside. When this is minced, it can cause bacteria to be mixed throughout the meat. Other meats, like pork and poultry, can have bacteria all the way through.

BUT WHAT DOES THIS MEAN FOR ME?

How different meats carry bacteria affect how they can or should be cooked. You can eat meats that have bacteria only on the outside 'rare' or pink, provided they have been sealed all the way around. Things like:

Beef steaks / Whole joints of beef /

Lamb chops / Whole joints of lamb

To seal a piece of meat, heat a large pan with some oil, season the meat well with salt and pepper, place it onto the hot pan and seal (get heat) on all sides in order to kill any bacteria that might be on the outside. You'll know the meat has been properly sealed when all of the outside has changed colour.

For larger cuts of meat, like rib roasts, after sealing they should be placed in the oven to cook further, but when it comes to things like steak all you need to do is seal it and leave on your pan until it's cooked to your liking.

Pro tip for pieces of meat like this: always leave them out of the fridge for a little while before cooking so that they reach room temperature.

WHICH MEATS SHOULD BE COOKED ALL THE WAY THROUGH?

It's essential to cook any meat that has been minced all of the way through. This applies to:

Rolled joints / Burgers / Sausages

Alongside this, poultry (chicken, turkey, duck) and pork also need to be cooked all the way through as these can have bacteria throughout.

When roasting the following guide is a really useful one to have to hand.

Meat	Time/Weight	Temperature
Whole chicken	20 mins per lb plus 20 extra mins	180°C/350°F
Pork joint	35 mins per lb plus 35 extra mins	180°C/350°F
Rolled joint	35 mins per lb plus 35 extra mins	180°C/350°F

HOW DO I CHECK THESE MEATS ARE PROPERLY COOKED?

When you pierce the thickest part of the meat with a fork or skewer, the juices should run clear. For a whole chicken, the thickest part is the leg between the drumstick and the breast. For other meats, it should be piping hot the whole way through, so make an incision to check. Meat changes colour when it is cooked, so make sure there is no pink meat left.

If you're cooking a very large dish, check it in a few places, because some parts of the dish may be less hot than others.

Don't forget the importance of resting your meat too. After cooking and before slicing/serving meat should be allowed to rest. This allows the juices to be reabsorbed into the meat; if you skip out on this you'll lose a tonne of the delicious juices when the meat is cut and it won't be as soft and juicy as you would like. It can be hard when you're excited to dig in and try what you've made, but trust me those couple of minutes make all of the difference to the end dish.

FISH

One of the most important things to note when it comes to cooking fish is to make sure that you wash it before you cook it, to make sure there is no salt water residue on it. Similarly, ensure that you wash your hands thoroughly before and after touching it.

Once you have chosen your fish, there are so many different ways you can cook it:

- Grilling
- Frying
- Roasting
- Baking
- Poaching
- Steaming

The easiest and healthiest way to cook fish is to bake it with a little bit of lemon juice, a splash of oil and some fresh herbs.

1. Preheat your oven to 200°C / 400°F.

2. Rinse the fish, and pat dry with some kitchen paper.

3. Drizzle the fillets with some olive oil, and season with salt and black pepper.

4. Place each fillet on a large piece of tinfoil, scatter with your choice of fresh herbs and a squeeze of lemon.

5. Carefully seal all edges of the tinfoil to form little parcels and place on a baking tray.

6. Bake in the oven for 15–20 minutes, depending on the size of fish.

Being able to make your own stock is such a great skill to have. You get such a delicious flavour from homemade stock, plus it is perfect for using up veggies you have lying around.

Ingredients:
1 small onion
1 parsnip
2 carrots
2 celery stalks
Handful of fresh parsley
2 bay leaves broken in half
2 cups of water

Method:
1. Roughly chop all of the vegetables and place in a large pot with the parsley and bay leaves.
2. Add the water and bring to the boil.
3. Once boiling, add a lid and simmer for 30 minutes.
4. Allow to cool fully before straining the mixture and removing the vegetables and herbs.

* Don't let anything go to waste: remove the herbs from the veg and you have a delicious bowl of boiled veg for lunch.

* If you want to make the flavour more intense place the broth back on your hob on a rolling boil for 20 minutes after you remove the solids.

* To make this recipe into chicken stock all you have to do is add some chicken bones, some thighs you have lying around, a leftover carcass from a roast or wing tips you were going to throw out – they will all taste delicious in a stock! The same instructions apply, just ensure if using raw chicken that it is fully cooked; you can remove it when removing the vegetables. You can use this same method for beef or fish stock too.

You just can't beat homemade nut butter, it's the best! The method is the same no matter your choice of nuts or the quantity you have. I tend to make mine in batches of 300–500g and above.

Method:
1. Preheat your oven to 180°C / 350°F.
2. Place the nuts on a baking tray and cook in the oven for 10 minutes until golden.
3. Once cooked, remove and leave to cool to room temperature.
4. Once they have cooled, place them in a food processor and blend for around 15 minutes until a smooth mixture forms, adding in some salt at the end.

You can keep nut butter in an airtight container for 1–2 weeks. There are endless possibilities for what nuts to use, along with different flavourings to add.

When it comes to homemade nut milks (or mylks if you prefer) I'm not really as passionate about making my own; there are some really great ones on the market with no additives so I tend to pick these up in my weekly shop. Nevertheless, it's always good to be able to make your own versions of things and also to have the knowledge of where your food comes from/how it's prepared.

To make homemade nut milk you will need:

1 cup of raw, unsalted cashews, or any raw nuts without skins
2 cups of water, plus more for soaking
Honey, agave or maple syrup (optional)

Method:
1. Place the nuts in a bowl and cover with about 1 inch of water. Cover them with a cloth and let sit overnight at room temperature. (The longer the nuts soak, the creamier the milk will be.)
2. Once they have had time to soak, drain the nuts and rinse them thoroughly under cool running water.
3. Add the nuts to your food processor along with 2 cups of fresh water.
4. Pulse the mixture a couple of times to break up the nuts before blending continuously on high for about 3 minutes. The nuts should be broken down into a very fine meal, and the water should be white and opaque.
5. Strain the milk through a nut milk bag or muslin cloth and pour into a jar for storage.
6. If you like your nut milk a little on the sweet side, add 1–2 tablespoons of your chosen sweetener – I recommend tasting first though.

You can keep your homemade nut milk in the fridge for 3–5 days; if it separates, just give it a quick shake to recombine. (I actually shake all nut milk before I use it, especially coconut. ☺)

HOW TO SEASON YOUR FOOD

One of the most important things when it comes to cooking is seasoning! I really can't stress this enough – it can make or break a dish. You'll see that I use a pinch of coarse salt in almost every recipe – which might get you thinking, is that healthy? I thought salt was bad? Why is she telling me to do that?

Well, let me bust a few myths for you when it comes to the use of salt. Similar to the war on fat, salt has developed a bad reputation over the years. The fact of the matter is that your body needs salt in order to function. Highly processed foods tend to have high quantities of salt, meaning that if you eat a lot of processed foods you are already likely to be getting enough, if not too much, salt in your diet as it is. On the other hand, when your diet is centred around whole, natural and unrefined/unprocessed foods there is then a need to ensure that you are getting enough of a salt intake. But seasoning doesn't just start and end with salt …

So what exactly is seasoning? Seasoning is all about enhancing the flavour of your food through the addition of salt, acidity, sugar, herbs and spices.

There are different types of seasoning depending on the cuisine but on a basic level it all boils down to salt, lemon and sugar.

COARSE SALT IS KING

First things first, it's important to get your hands on some good-quality coarse sea salt. Especially when it comes to seasoning meat, coarse salt has larger particles that distribute better and stick to the meat's surface.

ACIDITY BRINGS OUT A POP OF FLAVOUR

In addition to adding salt to boost flavour in soups, stews, sauces, etc. try a drop of lemon juice or vinegar.

SUGAR OFFSETS TARTNESS

I always add a little bit of sweetness when I'm cooking with a lot of tomatoes; a teaspoon or so of honey usually does the job.

WHEN IT COMES TO PEPPER – IT'S ALL ABOUT THE TIMING

Whether you season your meat with pepper before or after searing will affect the level of flavour that comes through.

If you're looking for a really, really strong peppery flavour, sprinkle over your meat after searing as keeping pepper away from heat preserves its volatile compounds, therefore creating a stronger flavour. Whereas if you sprinkle the pepper on the meat beforehand, it will tone down slightly during the cooking process.

COLD V HOT FOOD

You'll probably be surprised to know that chilling foods dulls the flavour slightly so it's important to season cold food a little more generously in order to bring out the flavour.

FOR HERBS IT'S ALL ABOUT TIMING

Hearty/strong herbs like thyme, rosemary, oregano and sage can be added to dishes early on in the cooking process. Save delicate herbs like parsley, coriander and basil until the last minute, otherwise they will lose their flavour, structure and colour.

A LITTLE UMAMI GOES A LONG WAY

When it comes to seasoning large dishes like a shepherd's pie, they can be transformed by things like Worcestershire sauce as an added seasoning.

ADD A FINISHING TOUCH

Even the most perfect of dishes can benefit from a last-minute burst of flavour. This could be in the form of one last sprinkle of salt to finish off, or when it comes to something like pan-fried fish or a steak, finishing it off by 'monte au beurre' is the way to go! Simply swirl a little bit of herby butter around the pan before you take the fish or steak off the pan – you can thank me later.

HOW TO SAFELY REHEAT YOUR FOOD

When it comes to how you handle leftovers, the process begins right at the time of cooking.

Ideally, leftovers should be placed in the fridge within 90 minutes of cooking, provided they have fully cooled. First things first, transfer the food out of any hot pots/pans/trays and move away from the heat source so that it's not being kept warm through any residual heat.

Food should be thoroughly cooled before putting it in the fridge/freezer, otherwise you risk increasing the temperature in your fridge and creating an environment where bacteria could multiply.

If you plan on eating your leftovers within the next day or two, place them in the fridge.

If there's a large quantity that you're not going to get through in two days, portion it up and freeze it as soon as it's cooled.

When it comes to heating up your leftovers, how you handle them is the key to staying safe and healthy. If you're taking leftovers from the freezer, defrost and eat them within 24 hours. It's also vital that you make sure whatever it is has thoroughly defrosted before heating.

You can't reheat leftovers more than once so be smart about how/when you do this.

If you have a big pot of something like chilli or soup, take out what you need and reheat it in smaller quantities.

It's super important that you reheat food until it's piping hot. Microwaves don't heat evenly so if you are reheating in your microwave be sure to take your food out halfway through and give it a stir/flip it over.

I cannot stress enough the importance of ensuring that leftovers are heated thoroughly and the whole way through. In general, all food should be heated until it reaches and maintains 70°C / 160°F or above for about 2 minutes.

KEY PANTRY ITEMS

Key cupboard ingredients to have on hand – basics that I always have on hand outside of the weekly shop. ☺

I'm regularly asked what's in my cupboard, along with why I use different ingredients, so I've put together this list with all of my cupboard staples that you will find in my house any day of the week.

HERBS AND SPICES

- Bay leaves
- Cardamom pods
- Cayenne pepper
- Chinese 5 spice
- Chipotle chilli flakes
- Cinnamon sticks
- Cloves
- Coarse sea salt
- Coriander leaf
- Coriander seeds
- Cumin seeds
- Curry powder
- Fennel seeds
- Garam masala
- Garlic granules
- Ground cinnamon
- Ground coriander
- Ground cumin
- Ground ginger
- Hot chilli flakes
- Italian herbs
- Kaffir lime leaves
- Mixed herbs
- Mustard seeds
- Normal paprika
- Nutmeg
- Oregano
- Parsley
- Peppercorns
- Piri-piri seasoning
- Rosemary
- Sage
- Smoked paprika
- Sumac
- Thyme
- Turmeric

FRESH ESSENTIALS

- Chilli
- Fresh basil
- Fresh coriander
- Fresh mint
- Fresh parsley
- Fresh rosemary
- Fresh thyme
- Garlic
- Ginger
- Onions
- Shallots
- Spring onions

STORE CUPBOARD ITEMS

- Agave
- Apple cider vinegar
- Assorted raw nuts: cashews, almonds, pistachios, pecans, walnuts
- Balsamic vinegar
- Butter
- Butter beans
- Cacao nibs
- Cacao powder
- Capers

- Chia seeds
- Chickpeas
- Coconut aminos
- Coconut cream
- Coconut milk
- Coconut oil
- Coconut sugar
- Desiccated coconut
- Dijon mustard
- English mustard
- Flaked almonds
- Flaxseeds
- Gelatine
- Ghee
- Ground almonds
- Harissa paste
- Honey
- Hot sauce
- Kidney beans
- Maple syrup
- Molasses
- Nut butter
- Nut milk
- Oats
- Olive oil
- Pine nuts
- Poppy seeds
- Pumpkin seeds
- Quinoa
- Sesame oil
- Sesame seeds
- Stevia
- Sunflower seeds
- Tahini
- Tinned tomatoes
- Tinned fruits (e.g. pears)
- Tomato passata
- Tomato purée
- Vanilla extract
- Vanilla pods
- Vegetable bouillon
- Worcestershire sauce
- Wholegrain mustard

DEATH ROW SUNDRIES

Woah that's a long list – what can you absolutely not live without?

First and foremost, I cannot stress enough the importance of building up a *good spice drawer*. My dessert island spices would be cumin, smoked paprika, garam masala, garlic granules and oregano – not a day goes by where I don't use one if not all of these.

OLIVE, COCONUT AND SESAME OIL

In order of appearance – olive is my go-to for 99% of things; it can be used in absolutely everything and I love how you can infuse flavours into it. Coconut is really great in desserts when you're substituting for things like butter – the consistency is great and I love the flavour. Sesame is my go-to for Asian flavours; it's rich, nutty and delicious.

FRANK'S HOT SAUCE

There is no magical reason for this – I adore it and cannot live without it; it's great with zoodles, added to burgers or in its natural habitat – chicken wings!

TINNED TOMATOES

I always have tinned tomatoes in the press; they are the basis of so many great recipes from baked eggs right through to spag bol.

COCONUT MILK

Coconut milk is the perfect addition to curries to get that thick, delicious creamy effect. I cannot stress enough the importance of full-fat coconut milk – it's the only way and always check your labels to make sure that it is just made up of coconut and water – no added nasties!

COCONUT AMINOS

A substitute I use in place of soy sauce. It's a soy-free alternative that is a blend of organic coconut tree sap aged and sun-dried mineral-rich sea salt, giving it a salty flavour that is also slightly sweet on the palate. If you're not a massive coconut fan don't worry because it doesn't taste like it at all.

ALMOND MILK

Of all of the nut milks, almond is my number 1. It's great with oats as well as adding to sauces. I tend to stick to unsweetened and opt for brands with no added preservatives.

OATS

Porridge is my absolute go-to when it comes to morning rituals. Even though oats are naturally gluten free they often get contaminated by other grains in the growing process so I always go for oats that are certified gluten free.

GROUND ALMONDS

Ground almonds are a great swap for flour/breadcrumbs. I always go for these rather than almond flour as they work just as well and are far more economical when it comes to the price tag.

CACAO POWDER

When it comes to baking cacao powder gives you the most chocolatey taste possible – I adore it. It comes from the cacao bean and is raw, unprocessed and extremely rich in nutrients.

MAPLE SYRUP

My preferred sweetener out of them all! I always opt for grade A.

DATES

Of all dried fruits dates are without a doubt my favourite – they're so delicious and high in fibre, which is key for good digestive health. I tend to use them most in energy balls and for me it has to be Medjool.

DARK CHOCOLATE

I buy good-quality high-percentage dark chocolate to snack on and use in my recipes. 65% is the absolute lowest I'll go but really 70–85% is the sweet spot.

FOOD MEASUREMENTS

Grams, cups, oz – what do they all mean anyway?

Personally, I'm not sold on any one metric when it comes to measuring things out – I tend to go between grams and cups with a few tablespoons/teaspoons thrown in here and there.

The below chart is a great reference point if you ever need to work something out when it comes to grams vs ounces.

Cup measures are a little different as it depends on what is being measured – there is no direct like-for-like table that can convert equal cup measures to grams or ounces. I really recommend, if you can, that you pick up a set of cup measures in your local supermarket.

See below as a guide for liquids:

Metric – Grams	Imperial – Oz
10g	¼ oz
15g	½ oz
25g	1 oz
30g	1 ¾ oz
50g	1 ¾ oz
75g	2 ¾ oz
100g	3 ½ oz
150g	5 ½ oz
175g	6 oz
200g	7 oz
225g	8 oz
250g	9 oz
275g	9 ¾ oz
300g	10 ½ oz
350g	12 oz
375g	13 oz
400g	14 oz
425g	15 oz
500g	1lb 2 oz
750g	1lb 10 oz
1kg	2 ¼ lb

Cup	Ml
1/4 cup	60ml
1/3 cup	80ml
1/2 cup	125ml
3/4 cup	160ml
1 cup	250ml

RECIPES

BREAKFAST

QUICK AND EASY PORRIDGE – 5 WAYS

I absolutely adore oats; they are a fantastic cupboard staple to have on hand to start your day. By changing them up each day, via your toppings or the milk that you prepare them with, it keeps things super varied and ensures you never get sick of them.

First up you can't go wrong with plain and simple oats, loaded with all of your favourite toppings! I typically go for around 40–50g of oats per person; it yields a nice hearty portion.

200ml is the liquid guide for all of the recipes below but feel free to increase depending on how your oats are looking on the day.

Per serving:
Plain and simple
40g oats
200ml water
(15g chia seeds optional)

My favourite toppings:
15g maple syrup
15g nut butter
1 square of dark chocolate
Generous helping of berries –
    raspberries are my go-to!

1. Combine the oats, chia seeds (if using) and water together in a small pot and place on a medium to high heat, stirring occasionally for 5–6 minutes until it comes to a gentle boil.
2. Reduce the heat to a simmer and cook for a further 2–3 minutes, stirring regularly, until cooked to your liking.
3. Serve and enjoy with your choice of toppings.

Other variations:
Stewed Apple Oats
40g oats
200ml almond milk

Toppings:
1 apple, peeled and chopped
1/2 tsp cinnamon
15g maple syrup
Handful of pecans
Handful of raisins

1. Place the apple in a small pot with a dash of water and allow to stew for about 10 minutes on a low heat until it has cooked through.
2. Combine the oats and almond milk together in a small pot and add to a medium to high heat, stirring occasionally for 5–6 minutes until it comes to a gentle boil.
3. Reduce the heat and cook for a further 2–3 minutes, stirring regularly, until cooked to your liking.
4. Place the porridge in a bowl with the stewed apple on top, scatter over the remaining toppings, serve and enjoy.

Porridge with Sticky Fried Banana

40g oats
200ml hazelnut milk

Toppings:
1 banana, sliced
1/2 tbsp grassfed butter
25g maple syrup
Handful of hazelnuts

1. Combine the oats and hazelnut milk together in a small pot and add to a medium to high heat, stirring occasionally for 5–6 minutes until it comes to a gentle boil.
2. Reduce the heat and cook for a further 2–3 minutes, stirring regularly, until cooked to your liking.
3. In the meantime, heat a pan with the butter and lightly fry the banana for 1–2 minutes per side until nice and golden; before taking off the heat drizzle with some maple syrup and toss the banana until coated.
4. Place the porridge in a bowl, add the banana on top and scatter with the hazelnuts and another drizzle of maple syrup. Enjoy.

Apple and Blackberry Oats

40g oats
200ml almond milk
15g flaxseeds
1/2 grated apple

Toppings:
Small handful blackberries
15g maple syrup

1. Combine the oats, flaxseeds and almond milk together with the grated apple in a small pot and add to a medium to high heat, stirring occasionally for 5–6 minutes until it comes to a gentle boil.
2. Reduce the heat and cook for a further 2–3 minutes, stirring regularly, until cooked to your liking.
3. Serve and enjoy with a handful of blackberries and a drizzle of maple syrup.

Gooey Chocolate Oats

40g oats
200ml almond milk
1 tsp cacao powder

Toppings:
15g maple syrup
15g almond butter
Large handful of toasted almonds, roughly chopped
1 square of chocolate (or more if you fancy!)

1. Combine the oats and almond milk together with cacao powder in a small pot and add to a medium to high heat, stirring occasionally for 5–6 minutes until it comes to a gentle boil.
2. Reduce the heat and cook for a further 2–3 minutes, stirring regularly, until cooked to your liking.
3. Serve and enjoy with your choice of chocolatey toppings scattered over the top.

BAKED OATS WITH BLACKBERRIES AND LEMON ZEST

I absolutely adore baking oats and love nothing more than waking up on a Saturday morning, rolling out of bed and whipping up a batch of them. To me there is no better way to kick-start the weekend. I'm constantly experimenting with different combinations!

Serves 1

50g oats
1 medium egg
6–8 blackberries
Juice and zest of 1/2 lemon
80ml water
1 tbsp agave (or sweetener of your choice)
1 tsp coconut oil

1. Preheat your oven to 180°C / 350°F.
2. In a small bowl add the egg, lemon juice, zest, water and agave and whisk until combined before stirring in the oats.
3. Grease a small ovenproof dish with the coconut oil.
4. Pour the oat mixture into the dish and pop the blackberries on top.
5. Bake in the oven for 20–25 minutes until the oats are fully cooked and cake-like.
6. Serve and enjoy; you can take this recipe to the next level by serving with an extra drizzle of agave and some runny nut butter!

GRAB AND GO BANANA MUFFINS

The best thing about this recipe is that you can literally pop everything into your mixer and it's done! I like to use mini loaf tins; however muffin cases work great too.

They freeze really well too so feel free to double up on the recipe ☺

Serves 8

4 ripe bananas
100g oats
110g ground almonds
4 eggs
1 tsp vanilla extract
100g coconut oil
1 tsp baking powder
1 tsp all spice
1 tsp cinnamon
6 tbsp agave

1. Preheat your oven to 180°C / 350°F.
2. Mash 3 of the bananas and add to your mixer with the remainder of the ingredients and mix until combined.
3. Separate the mixture out evenly into loaf tins.
4. Slice the remaining banana and place a couple of slices on top of each of the loaves before adding to the oven to bake for 30 minutes until golden brown and cooked through. Allow to cool slightly before serving!

BAKED EGGS WITH TOMATOES AND PEPPERS

Baked eggs are an incredibly simple way of creating an impressive-looking breakfast for your loved ones. I love preparing them on Sunday mornings and enjoying them while I read through the weekend magazines.

Serves 2

1 shallot, finely diced
1 x 400g tin of chopped tomatoes
1/2 tsp garlic granules
2 tsp Italian herbs
Large pinch of chipotle chilli flakes
2 large handfuls (100g) spinach
60g grilled peppers (see recipe p. 193)
3 eggs
1/2 tsp your chosen oil
Coarse sea salt and cracked black
    pepper

1. Preheat your oven to 200°C / 400°F.
2. In a large ovenproof frying pan, heat the oil and gently sauté the shallot for 1–2 minutes until it has become translucent.
3. Stir in the chopped tomatoes followed by the garlic, Italian herbs and chipotle flakes.
4. Allow the mixture to cook for 2–3 minutes before stirring in the spinach and cooking for a further minute.
5. Once the spinach has wilted, remove the pan from the heat and crack in the eggs.
6. Scatter over the grilled peppers and season with some coarse sea salt and cracked black pepper.
7. Bake in the oven for 10–12 minutes until the eggs are cooked to your liking, serve and enjoy!

BRUNCH BOWL

This recipe was inspired by a breakfast I had on a trip to London; we stopped off in Balthazar's and I had their breakfast salad. It was absolutely stunning and led to the inspiration for this brunch bowl, which has fast become one of my staple late-Saturday-morning meals.

Serves 1

1 large handful of mixed leaves
45g quinoa, cooked
50g bacon lardons
1 large handful of baby kale
1 large handful of baby spinach
8–10 cherry tomatoes, sliced in half
1/4 – 1/2 tsp Tabasco sauce
1 egg
1/4 avocado, diced
1/2 tsp your chosen oil
Coarse sea salt and cracked black
    pepper

1 tsp pumpkin seeds, 1/2 tsp flaxseeds,
    1/2 tsp linseeds, to garnish

1. Add the lardons to a dry cold pan and begin to cook over a high heat.
2. Once the lardons are fully cooked and nice and crispy, add the quinoa to the pan and stir well; cook for 2–3 minutes until the quinoa has begun to heat up.
3. Next, add the tomatoes, spinach, kale and Tabasco and mix thoroughly.
4. Reduce the heat and cook for 3–4 minutes until the tomatoes are cooked through and the spinach and kale are nicely wilted.
5. In the meantime, heat another pan with some oil and fry the egg to your liking.
6. Finally, add the mixed leaves to a bowl, followed by the quinoa mix, before adding the avocado and fried egg, finishing with a sprinkle of seeds, coarse sea salt and some cracked black pepper.
7. Serve and enjoy!

SWEET POTATO CAKES WITH SMOKED SALMON

As a child, potato cakes and smoked salmon used to be one of my favourite midweek dinners. My mum would use leftover mashed potatoes to create her signature recipe; this is an adaptation of a classic which is sensational alongside some sautéed greens and poached eggs.

Serves 3–4

3 large sweet potatoes, peeled and cut into large chunks
A generous knob of grassfed butter
1/4 cup of ground almonds
3 tbsp coconut flour
3–4 slices of smoked salmon per person to serve
Coarse sea salt and cracked black pepper

1. Boil or steam the sweet potatoes until tender, about 10–15 minutes.
2. Once cooked through and nice and soft, set aside to cool slightly.
3. To make the potato cakes, mash the sweet potato and stir in the ground almonds and butter with a generous amount of coarse sea salt and cracked black pepper.
4. Combine until it has formed a dough-like ball.
5. Dust a chopping board or your countertop with the coconut flour.
6. Split up the dough and roll out into little cakes.
7. Place the potato cakes onto a cold dry pan, turn up the heat and cook for 6–8 minutes per side until golden and heated through.
8. Serve and enjoy with a generous portion of smoked salmon and some added butter.

RASPBERRY RIPPLE OVERNIGHT OATS

Summer time is the perfect opportunity to change up your morning routine from porridge to overnight oats; they are perfect for grabbing on the go. Just like traditional porridge, the topping combinations are endless!

Serves 2

100g vanilla coconut yoghurt
15g chia seeds
15g flaxseeds
80g oats
2 tbsp agave
300ml almond milk
1 tsp vanilla extract
4 tbsp (or more!) of chia jam (see recipe p. 199)

50g raspberries, to garnish

1. Divide the coconut yoghurt between 2 serving bowls and place at the bottom.
2. Next, do the same with the chia jam and place it on top of the coconut yoghurt.
3. In a large bowl or jug combine the remaining ingredients and mix well before dividing between the two serving bowls.
4. Place in your fridge overnight and serve the next morning with the fresh raspberries on top.
5. Serve and enjoy!

RHUBARB BAKED OATS

When it comes into season rhubarb is sensational; make the most of it while you can by transforming your morning oats into this baked edition!

Serves 2

150g roasted rhubarb, sliced into chunks
2 eggs
90g oats
2 tsp vanilla extract
2 tbsp maple syrup
75ml water
75ml almond milk
1 tsp cinnamon
1/2 tsp coconut oil

1. Preheat your oven to 200°C / 400°F.
2. Lightly grease 2 ovenproof dishes with the coconut oil.
3. In a large jug/bowl, combine the remaining ingredients bar the rhubarb and mix thoroughly.
4. Divide the mixture between the 2 ovenproof dishes, scatted the rhubarb pieces on top and bake in the oven for 30–35 minutes until fully cooked.
5. Serve and enjoy with an extra drizzle of maple syrup.

CHIA PUDDING

I'll admit I was slow to convert to chia pudding, but I really think it was just down to not getting the quantities correct – once you have that nailed it's one of the best breakfasts ever!

Another great one for the summer months if you tire of porridge ☺

Serves 1

50g chia seeds
225ml unsweetened almond milk
1 tsp vanilla extract
2–3 tbsp stevia
125g raspberries

1. In a large bowl combine the chia seeds and stevia.
2. Pour in the almond milk and vanilla, mix thoroughly.
3. Add half of the raspberries and mix again.
4. Place the mixture in the fridge and allow to set overnight.
5. Serve and enjoy with the remaining raspberries.

ODE TO DAD'S SAUSAGE PATTIES

I absolutely adore Christmas time; without sounding cheesy it really is the most wonderful time of the year! Christmas dinner is my Dad's yearly showstopper. He does all the cooking himself and the highlight of this for me is his famous sausage patties. They began as a by-product of his sausage stuffing and very quickly soared to one of the most anticipated parts of the day. We have them for breakfast on Christmas morning and as many mornings throughout the Christmas period as our sausage meat supplies stretch to!

This recipe is an adaptation of a classic that can be enjoyed year-round.

Makes 8 patties, serves 4

500g lean pork mince
4 shallots, finely diced
40g ground almonds
1 large egg
1/2 tsp sage
1 tsp parsley
1 tsp thyme
3 cloves of garlic, minced
1 tsp your chosen oil
Coarse sea salt and cracked black
   pepper

1. Combine all of the ingredients bar the oil in a bowl and mix thoroughly before shaping into patties.
2. Heat a large frying pan with the oil and cook the patties on high for 1–2 minutes before reducing the heat and cooking for a further 3 minutes.
3. Increase the heat again and flip the patties, cook on high on the opposite side for 1–2 minutes before reducing the heat again.
4. Cook on low for an additional 3–4 minutes until the patties are fully cooked, serve and enjoy.

THE FAMOUS SCRAMBLED EGGS

There are very few people who can rival the Halloran family scrambled eggs – sit back and brace yourself, I'm about to let you in on the best-kept secret of all time!

Controversially, we use a microwave and even more controversially there is no exact science when it comes to the timing on this because everyone likes their eggs prepared to different levels of cooked. My best advice here is regular rigorous whisking of the eggs and quite literally standing over it until it is cooked.

Serves 4

6–8 eggs
Generous knob of grassfed butter
3 tbsp of water (or milk)
Good pinch of coarse sea salt and
  cracked black pepper

Optional:
At the end you can also stir in some sautéed veggies like tomatoes and spinach to bulk it out

1. In a large glass bowl add all of the ingredients and whisk vigorously until combined.
2. Place in your microwave and cook for 2 minutes.
3. Remove from the microwave and whisk thoroughly before placing back in again.
4. Continue cooking on 1-minute / 30-second cycles until it is almost cooked to your liking – at that point, remove (at speed!) from the microwave and start to serve as it will continue to cook away itself for a minute or so.
5. Serve and enjoy.

NICOLA'S TIP

To avoid messy clean-ups, once you serve the eggs fill the bowl you used to cook them in with cold water and allow to sit while you eat ... you can thank me later!

BREAKFAST HASH

This could be considered a slightly unorthodox breakfast choice but trust me once you hash you'll never go back. A great option for days when you're trying to come up with something that isn't oats or eggs.

Serves 2

300g turkey mince
250g baby potatoes, halved
200g sweet potato, cubed
200g Brussels sprouts, halved
200g spinach
70g grilled peppers (see recipe p. 193)
1 tsp piri-piri seasoning
1/2 tbsp Italian herb seasoning
1 tsp your chosen oil
Coarse sea salt and cracked black
  pepper

1. Begin by steaming the potatoes for 4–5 minutes until they begin to soften.
2. Heat the oil in a large pan, then add the potatoes to the pan to crisp with a pinch of coarse sea salt, cracked black pepper, piri-piri and Italian herb seasoning.
3. Next add the turkey mince to the pan and cook for 3–4 minutes.
4. In the meantime steam the sprouts for 3 minutes.
5. Add the sprouts to the pan and allow to brown.
6. Finally mix in the spinach; once it has begun to wilt remove the pan from the heat and plate up.
7. Scatter the grilled peppers on top, serve and enjoy!

QUICK AND EASY MIDDAY MEALS

THE WONKY SALAD –
HOW TO CREATE THE PERFECT SALAD

Sometimes salads get a bit of a bad rep for being the boring or obvious choice but what I hope you come away with after reading this next recipe is that this couldn't be further from the truth. The possibilities are endless when it comes to salads. I even enjoy them for breakfast – check out my brunch bowl on page 57.

LEAFY BASE	CARBS	FATS	PROTEIN	TOPPINGS	DRESSING
Cos/Iceberg	Roasted sweet potato cubes	Avocado	Chicken and bacon	Toasted pumpkin seeds	Balsamic
Mixed leaves	Quinoa	Green olives	Turkey burger	Grilled peppers and mixed seeds	Hot sauce
Spinach	Baby potatoes	Avocado	Baked salmon and prawns	Pine nuts and grilled peppers	Garlic and chilli oil
Rocket	Roasted veggies	Mixed nuts and sundried tomatoes	Fried egg	Griddled asparagus	Balsamic
Kale	Roasted cauliflower and broccoli	Toasted almonds	Roast chicken	Pickled cucumber and grapes	Almond butter drizzle

This chart shows examples of key ingredients that you can combine to build your own personal salad. These are just a few simple suggestions – the possibilities really are endless. Feel free to play around, you never know what might end up in your bowl!

CHICKEN FAJITA SOUP

There is just something so exotic about this warming soup. It makes you feel like you are on holidays – when in reality you're heating it on the go during a hectic day – but for those five minutes you can escape through your taste buds to warmer, more exciting places.

Serves 4–6

1.5kg tomatoes
2 peppers, sliced
1 red onion, diced
4 cloves of garlic, minced
450g chicken thighs
1 pint of chicken stock
400g butter beans
400g black beans
Olive oil
Coarse sea salt and cracked black
   pepper

Fajita seasoning:
1 tsp chilli powder
1 tsp garlic powder
1 tsp smoked paprika
1 tsp cumin
1 tsp oregano
1/4 tsp turmeric
1/4 tsp cinnamon

Pinch of chipotle flakes
Bunch of fresh coriander
Sliced avocado

1. Begin by roasting the tomatoes in a small drizzle of olive oil at 200°C / 400°F for 30 minutes.
2. Next, heat a large pot with a small drizzle of oil and sauté the peppers, onion and garlic for 3–5 minutes.
3. Add the remaining ingredients, including the fajita seasoning, and bring to the boil before reducing the heat and simmering for 20 minutes.
4. Remove the chicken from the pot, provided it's fully cooked; continue to cook the soup for a further 10–15 minutes until nice and thick.
5. Shred the chicken and stir it back in, finishing with a little sprinkle of chipotle flakes, a large bunch of fresh coriander and a final sprinkle of salt and pepper.
6. Serve and enjoy with some sliced avocado.

CREAMY MUSHROOM SOUP

A wonderfully hearty soup that hugs you from the inside out. If you can't get your hands on the mushroom variations feel free to just run with one type.

Serves 4–6

250g chestnut mushrooms
250g mini portobello mushrooms
250g button mushrooms
2 stalks of celery
1 onion
3 cloves of garlic, minced
1 tsp garlic and chilli oil (see p. 195)
1 tbsp Italian herb seasoning
1.5l chicken stock
100ml coconut milk
Coarse sea salt and cracked black
    pepper
Fresh parsley and toasted sesame
    seeds to garnish

1. Begin by slicing all of the vegetables into thin strips.
2. Heat a large pot with the oil and lightly sauté the onion, celery and garlic with a good pinch of salt and pepper for 1–2 minutes until the onion starts to become translucent.
3. Next add the mushrooms and sauté for 5–8 minutes until they are slightly golden.
4. Add the chicken stock and bring the mixture to the boil before simmering for 25–30 minutes.
5. Using a handheld blender, blitz until smooth before adding in the coconut milk.
6. Bring the soup back to a light boil and reduce to a simmer for 3–5 minutes until heated through.
7. Serve and enjoy with some fresh parsley and toasted sesame seeds.

ROASTED VEGGIE SOUP

I really try to avoid food waste as much as possible – this is great way to revitalise any vegetables that may have started to look a bit sad in the fridge, and to transform them into a hearty soup that can be kept in the fridge for up to a week or portioned out and stored in your freezer for up to six months.

Serves 6–8

4 peppers, diced
5 cloves of garlic, minced
2 leeks, diced
1 head of broccoli, separated into
    florets
4 carrots, peeled and sliced
4 stalks of celery, roughly chopped
2–3 tbsp of olive oil
Pinch of chipotle flakes
1 tsp ground coriander
1 tsp cumin
1.5l vegetable stock
Coarse sea salt and cracked black
    pepper

1. Preheat your oven to 200°C / 400°F.
2. Lay out the veggies on a large baking dish, toss in the olive oil and sprinkle with salt, pepper and spices.
3. Bake in the oven for 45–50 minutes, tossing occasionally.
4. Heat the stock in a large pot, remove the veggies from the oven and add to the stock.
5. Blend with your hand blender until smooth.
6. Bring the soup back to a light boil before reducing to a simmer for 3–5 minutes until heated through.
7. Serve and enjoy!

CHICKEN ZOODLE SOUP

This recipe is one of my favourite things to race home to, grab a big woolly blanket and cosy up on the couch with during colder months. Prepare the broth ahead of time and add in your zoodles as needed for comfort in a bowl any time of the day.

Serves 3–4

For the broth:
3 chicken thighs, skinned
3/4 of a carrot, peeled and chopped
1 small onion, peeled and chopped
2 stalks of celery, roughly chopped
1 handful of fresh parsley
1 handful of fresh thyme
2 cups of water – just enough to cover
    the vegetables
Coarse sea salt and cracked black
    pepper

For the zoodles:
1/4 of a carrot, peeled
1/2 a sweet potato, peeled
2 large courgettes
All spiralised

Small handful of fresh coriander to garnish

1. Add all of the broth ingredients to a large pot and season well.
2. Bring to the boil over a high heat, reduce the heat and simmer for 30–40 minutes with the lid on, until the chicken has cooked through.
3. Once the broth has finished cooking, remove the chicken and set aside, before straining the remainder of the mixture and discarding the vegetables.
4. Bring the broth to the boil and simmer for a further 5–10 minutes to enhance the flavour.
5. Once you are ready to serve your soup, tear the chicken away from the bones, add into the broth and simmer for 5 minutes.
6. Add the spiralised carrot and sweet potato and simmer for a further 5 minutes.
7. Turn off the hob, add the zoodles and leave to stand for 3–5 minutes with the lid on.
8. Garnish with coriander and enjoy snuggled up on the couch with a woolly blanket.
   The perfect way to relax after a busy day!

PESTO MUSSELS

I adore mussels, and have done for as far back as I can remember. They bring back such fond memories of tucking into them as a child in Sligo with my grandad. No trip was complete without at least one portion. Until very recently I had shied away from making them myself at home as I wasn't totally confident on how to cook them but it really couldn't be any simpler and you can do it in no time at all.

Serves 2

800g rope mussels, cleaned and in a
    bowl of fresh water
4 heaped tbsp of pesto (see recipe
    p. 197)
1 tsp olive oil
Coarse sea salt and cracked black
    pepper
Basil to garnish

1. Rinse the mussels in some fresh water, place in a bowl full of water and leave to sit for 4–5 minutes.
2. Pick through and discard any mussels at this point which are not closed, drain the water from the mussels and set aside.
3. Heat the olive oil in a large pan (one which will fit all of your mussels!)
4. Next add the pesto and cook for about a minute until it has heated through, before adding the mussels to the pan. Mix until coated in the pesto before placing the lid on the pan and cooking for 4–6 minutes, or until all of the mussels have opened. If any mussels are still unopened after cooking discard them.
5. Serve and enjoy garnished with some chopped basil.

CUCUMBER AND AVOCADO STACKS WITH SMOKED SALMON

These little bites are the perfect snack, packed full of flavour, and this recipe is super simple and all about the assembly process.

Serves 10–12

1 portion of the Ultimate Guacamole (see p. 191)
1 cucumber
6–8 slices of smoked salmon
Large bunch of fresh dill, roughly chopped

1. Begin by slicing the cucumber into discs.
2. Stack the cucumber with a spoonful of guac and add a small slice of smoked salmon on top.
3. Repeat this process until you have used up all of the ingredients, sprinkle over some chopped dill, serve and enjoy!

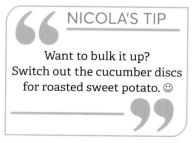

NICOLA'S TIP

Want to bulk it up?
Switch out the cucumber discs
for roasted sweet potato. ☺

BUDDHA BOWL

There's nothing I love more than a bowl piled high with delicious veggies – this is one of my go-to midday meals. It's pretty substantial but if you fancy it, don't be afraid to bulk it up further with some chicken, an egg or even a sprinkle of roasted nuts.

Outside of roasting the veggies it's really just an assembly piece so it's perfect to have prepped in advance.

Serves 1

1 small sweet potato, cut into cubes
200g Brussel sprouts, halved
1 tbsp olive oil
Large handful of spinach
1/2 avocado
2–3 radishes, thinly sliced
1 cooked beetroot, cubed
Handful of pomegranate seeds
2 heaping spoons of baba ghanoush
    (see p. 201)
Pinch of coarse sea salt and cracked
    black pepper

1. Preheat your oven to 200°C / 400°F.
2. Toss the sweet potato and sprouts in the olive oil before placing on a baking tray with a sprinkle of coarse sea salt and pepper.
3. Bake in the oven for 15–20 minutes until cooked to your liking.
4. Next, get yourself a large bowl and assemble! This is my favourite part – making everything look super pretty.
5. Serve and enjoy!

TURKEY TERIYAKI LETTUCE CUPS

What's not to love about this recipe? It's super quick and super tasty! I adore lettuce cups, they're one of my favourite vessels for food – whether it's as simple as a piece of parma ham or the recipe below, they're my go-to.

Serves 2–3

500g turkey mince (breast or thigh, whichever you prefer)
1 head of baby cos lettuce, separated into leaves
Sprinkle of sesame seeds
2 spring onions, finely chopped
Your chosen oil

For the sauce:
1/3 cup of honey
1/3 cup of coconut aminos
1 tbsp vinegar (either white wine or apple cider)
1 tbsp sesame oil
2 cloves of garlic, minced
1/2 red chilli, finely chopped
1/2 tbsp arrowroot powder

1. Whisk all of the sauce ingredients together and add them to a saucepan over a medium heat. Allow the mixture to come to the boil before reducing to a simmer for 8–10 minutes until it is nice and thick.
2. Heat 1 tsp of oil in a large pan or wok and brown the turkey mince for 5–8 minutes with a pinch of coarse sea salt.
3. Once it is almost fully cooked add the sauce and mix thoroughly.
4. Remove from the heat and plate up into lettuce cups with a sprinkle of sesame seeds and some spring onions. Enjoy!

ROLL-UP LETTUCE WRAPS

A super simple recipe that is all about the assembly!

Serves 1

Per lettuce wrap:
6–8 pieces of iceberg lettuce
1 handful of beansprouts
1/4 pepper, sliced
1/2 carrot grated
2–3 inches cucumber, sliced
1 chicken breast, cooked

You will also need:
Parchment paper and some string

1. Lay out a piece of parchment paper on your counter top.
2. On the parchment lay out the iceberg lettuce.
3. In the centre of the lettuce pile up the rest of the ingredients.
4. Finally, roll the lettuce into a burrito-like shape, wrap the parchment paper around it and tie with 2 pieces of string, side by side.
5. Slice and enjoy!

CHICKEN AND BACON SKEWERS

Chicken and bacon is always a winning combo! These skewers are the perfect party food, super simple to prepare and a total taste sensation.

Serves 3–4

350g chicken breast, sliced into strips
12 slices of streaky bacon

For the marinade:
2 tbsp honey
4 cloves of garlic, minced
1 tbsp sesame oil
4 tbsp coconut aminos
1 tbsp lime juice
1/2 jalapeño, finely diced
1/2 tbsp arrowroot powder
1 tbsp sesame seeds

1. Start by preheating your oven to 190°C / 375°F.
2. In a small saucepan combine all of the marinade ingredients bar the sesame seeds.
3. Whisk together and place over a medium heat. Allow the mixture to come to the boil before reducing to a simmer for 8–10 minutes until it is nice and thick.
4. Remove from the heat and allow to cool slightly.
5. Stir the sesame seeds into the sauce before adding to a large bowl with the chicken strips.
6. Line a baking tray with some baking paper and place a wire rack on top.
7. Place the chicken and bacon onto wooden skewers, beginning with the bacon and then weaving it over each strip of chicken as you layer them up and place on the wire rack.
8. Brush on any remaining marinade to the skewers before placing in the oven for 10–12 minutes until the chicken is fully cooked.
9. Place under a grill for a minute each side to crisp up the bacon. Serve and enjoy!

MINI SLIDERS

A great little recipe to have up your sleeve, it can be used with any mince: beef, pork, chicken, turkey, lamb … you name it! Lamb is my favourite for this combination, as is a mix of half beef, half lamb if you're feeling adventurous!

I like to cook these ones in the oven but they work great on a pan or BBQ too.

Makes 6–8, serves 3–4

500g of your choice of mince
1/2 onion, finely diced
2 cloves of garlic, minced
Zest of 1 lemon
Handful of chopped parsley
2 tsp ground cumin
1 tsp oregano
1/4 tsp cayenne pepper
Coarse sea salt and cracked black
    pepper

1. Preheat your oven to 200°C / 400°F.
2. In a large bowl combine all of the ingredients with the mince and season with coarse sea salt and cracked black pepper.
3. Roll into little golf-ball-sized sliders and place on an ovenproof dish.
4. Bake in the oven for 15–20 minutes until cooked through, serve and enjoy with your choice of sides!

SWEET POTATO TOAST

I am obsessed with sweet potato toast – it's so nutritious and filling plus the toppings are endless so you will never get bored. Prep in advance and reheat the sweet potato in your toaster, just like real toast!

Below is the recipe for smashed avocado – other combos I love are almond butter and strawberries, crispy bacon and an egg, as well as baba ghanoush (check out the recipe on p. 201) and pomegranate.

Serves 4

2 large sweet potatoes, skin on, cut
    into large slices
2 ripe avocados
Juice of one lime
1/2 tsp garlic powder
1/2 tsp of chilli powder or smoked
    paprika
Handful of cherry tomatoes, sliced
2 tbsp olive or coconut oil
Sprinkle of cracked black pepper

1. Preheat your oven to 220°C / 428°F.
2. Toss the sweet potato in your chosen oil and place on a baking dish.
3. Bake in the oven for 15–20 minutes until golden, flipping halfway through.
4. In a bowl smash the avocado, add in the lime juice, spices and tomatoes.
5. Remove the sweet potato from the oven and smother in guac, serve and enjoy with a sprinkle of cracked black pepper.

FISH CAKES
WITH ALFALFA SPROUTS

I adore these fish cakes – they were one of the very first things I tried my hand at making when I found my feet in the kitchen. They're great if you're looking to use up leftover fish or sweet potato; I also never shy away from making them from scratch.

Serves 4

2 sweet potatoes, peeled
1 tsp grassfed butter
1 tsp oregano
2 salmon darnes, baked in a little
    lemon juice, salt and pepper
1 red onion, finely chopped
1 large egg
2 tbsp ground almonds
Pinch of chipotle flakes
Zest of a lime
2 cloves of garlic, minced
1 box of alfalfa sprouts

1. First up, preheat your oven to 200°C / 400°F.
2. Begin by steaming the sweet potatoes for 8–10 minutes until nice and soft.
3. Next, mash them together with the butter and the oregano.
4. Flake the salmon into the bowl and add the rest of the ingredients, except the alfalfa sprouts.
5. Mix thoroughly and then shape into patties.
6. Place on a greased baking sheet and bake for 15 minutes or until golden and heated through, flipping over for the last 2–3 minutes.
7. Serve and enjoy with a large handful of alfalfa sprouts.

MINTY LAMB MEATBALLS

A little while ago I was challenged to come up with a meatball recipe that had an Irish twist; lamb and mint sauce felt like the perfect fit and these beauties were born. It's super simple and a total crowd pleaser!

Serves 4

500g lamb mince
1 small onion, finely diced
4 cloves of garlic, minced
Handful of fresh mint leaves, roughly
    chopped
2 tbsp paprika
2 tsp ground cumin
Large pinch of coarse sea salt
1/4 tsp cayenne pepper (optional)

Your chosen oil for cooking
Mint sauce to serve

1. In a large bowl combine all of the ingredients.
2. Form into meatballs; this recipe yields about 8.
3. Heat a large frying pan with some oil until piping hot, and add about 4 meatballs to the pan; you don't want to overcrowd them.
4. Cook in batches for 4 minutes a side (8 in total) until golden and cooked through.
5. Serve with some mint sauce and enjoy.

MAINS
HEARTY EVENING MEALS

CHICKEN AND BROCCOLI BAKE

I am all about comfort food and this chicken and broccoli bake is the ultimate comfort food. It's a serious crowd pleaser and makes for the best ever leftovers. It works just great with all parts of the chicken, whether you want to go whole chicken or try out legs/thighs – whatever you have on hand, so feel free to play around.

Serves 4–6

4 chicken breasts, sliced into strips
1 large onion, sliced
2 carrots, peeled and sliced
2 stalks of celery, sliced
1 head of broccoli, separated into
    florets
200g creamed coconut
1 bay leaf
1 clove of garlic, minced
1 large handful of parsley
1 tbsp arrowroot powder

For the crust:
1/2 cup ground almonds
1/2 cup oats
1 tbsp dried thyme
3 tbsp mixed seeds
1/2 tbsp dried parsley
1 tbsp grassfed butter

1. Preheat your oven to 180°C / 350°F.
2. In a large saucepan add the chicken, onions, carrots, celery, parsley and bay leaf and fill with water until everything is nicely covered.
3. Slowly bring the mixture to the boil before reducing to a simmer for 25–30 minutes.
4. Strain the cooking liquid into a smaller saucepan and bring to the boil until it has reduced down to about 1 pint of liquid.
5. In the meantime, place the chicken and vegetables in an ovenproof dish and set aside while you prepare the broccoli.
6. Next, blanch the broccoli in boiling water for 5–7 minutes until tender; remove from the water, refresh under cold water, and add to the ovenproof dish with the chicken and vegetables.
7. Once the broth has reduced, stir in the creamed coconut and allow the mixture to heat through before adding the arrowroot powder to thicken.
8. Pour the sauce over the chicken and vegetables, giving it a good mix to ensure everything is generously coated in the sauce.
9. Finally, to make the crust, melt the butter and mix with all of the topping ingredients, then spread evenly over the chicken mixture before placing in the oven.
10. Bake in the oven for 15–20 minutes.

RED HOT TURKEY BURGERS

I love turkey burgers and I love hot sauce so for me this is a total match made in heaven. Best done on a griddle pan to get those all-important char lines!

Serves 4

400g turkey mince
1/2 red onion, finely diced
1/2 green pepper, finely diced
3 cloves of garlic, minced
Handful of fresh coriander leaves
1/4 green chilli, finely diced
Handful of fresh coriander leaves
Small pinch of cumin, chipotle flakes
　and ground coriander
2 tbsp Frank's Red Hot Sauce
Coarse sea salt

1 tsp olive oil, for cooking

1. In a large bowl combine the turkey mince and all of the other ingredients with a sprinkle of coarse sea salt.
2. Shape the mixture into patties; this recipe yields 4.
3. Heat your pan with a good drizzle of olive oil (approx 1 tsp) and cook the burgers for 4–6 minutes a side until fully cooked.
4. Serve and enjoy, it really couldn't be easier.

COTTAGE PIE WITH PARSNIP MASH

This is a dish that brings back such fond memories of growing up – it's a super winter warmer and the ultimate definition of comfort food. This recipe is a play on my mum's signature dish; don't get me wrong, I'm not opposed to using potatoes but it's always nice to put your own spin on things and for me the parsnip does just that.

Serves 4–6

500g lean beef mince
4 stalks of celery, cubed
2 carrots, peeled and cubed
1 large Spanish onion, diced
3 cloves of garlic, minced
200g mushrooms, thinly sliced
2 tbsp Worchester sauce
1 tbsp Italian herb seasoning
500ml rich beef stock
5 large parsnips, peeled and chopped
1 tbsp grassfed butter
1 egg
1 tsp olive oil
Coarse sea salt and cracked black
    pepper

1. Preheat your oven to 200°C / 400°F.
2. In a large pan heat the olive oil and sauté the onion for 2–3 minutes until it starts to become translucent.
3. Next add the celery, carrots, garlic, herbs and a pinch of salt and pepper to the pan and sauté for a further 5 minutes before adding the contents to a large saucepan.
4. Add another small dash of olive oil to the pan and brown the mince for 4–5 minutes before adding to the saucepan.
5. Lightly, sauté the mushrooms and add to the saucepan with the stock and Worchester sauce.
6. Bring the mixture to the boil, cover and simmer for 25–30 minutes.
7. In the meantime boil the parsnips for 10–15 minutes until tender. Remove from the heat and strain before mashing.
8. Take the pie mix off the heat and transfer to an ovenproof dish.
9. Beat in the egg and butter to the parsnip mash and season with salt and pepper.
10. Cover the pie mixture with the parsnip mash and press down with a fork.
11. Place in the oven for 20–25 minutes, until the top is starting to brown and the mince is bubbling through at the edges.
12. Remove from the oven and allow to cool slightly before serving. ☺ Enjoy!

PAN-FRIED SEA BASS WITH PROVENÇALE VEGETABLES

Sea bass is one of my favourite fish to cook. It crisps up so wonderfully and is packed full of flavour. The veggies alongside this are a super addition which will transport you to a sunny port in the Mediterranean from the very first bite.

Serves 2

1 aubergine, sliced into chunks
2 courgettes, diced
Large handful of mushrooms, sliced
Large handful of cherry tomatoes
1 pepper, diced
2 cloves of garlic, minced
Small handful of fresh basil, finely
    chopped
1 tsp Herbes de Provence
Large sprinkle of coarse sea salt and
    cracked black pepper
1–2 tbsp olive oil

For the fish:
2 fillets of sea bass per person
1 tbsp olive oil

1. Preheat your oven to 200°C / 400°F.
2. In a large ovenproof dish, lay out the veggies and toss in the seasoning and oil.
3. Bake in the oven for 25–30 minutes until fully cooked, turning regularly.
4. Heat a large frying pan until hot then add 1 tablespoon of olive oil.
5. Season the fish, place it into the pan skin side down and cook for 4–5 minutes until almost cooked through and the skin is golden and crispy.
6. Flip onto the opposite side, reduce the temperature and continue to cook for a further 2–3 minutes until cooked all the way through.
7. Serve and enjoy with the veggies!

SWEET POTATO GNOCCHI WITH LEMON, PINE NUTS AND SAGE BUTTER

This is one of those recipes that will make you do a happy dance around the kitchen once you try it – the ultimate comfort food.

Serves 6–8

800g sweet potato, peeled and cut into
    wedges
1 tbsp olive oil
2 cups of ground almonds (200g)
1 cup arrowroot powder (60g)
1 cup coconut flour (60g)
1/2 tsp garlic granules
1 tsp baking soda
1 egg
150g grassfed butter
Large handful of fresh sage leaves
4 cloves of garlic
Juice of 1/2 lemon
Zest of 1 lemon
Large handful toasted pine nuts
Pinch of coarse sea salt and cracked
    black pepper

1. Lay the sweet potato on a baking tray, drizzle with olive oil and sprinkle with some coarse sea salt and cracked black pepper.
2. Bake the sweet potato in the oven at 200°C / 400°F for 15 minutes until tender.
3. Remove from the oven and mash before allowing to cool slightly.
4. Once the mash has cooled down add to a large bowl and combine with the ground almonds, arrowroot powder, coconut flour, garlic granules and baking soda.
5. Next beat the egg and combine thoroughly until all the ingredients form a nice ball.
6. Place in the fridge to chill for a couple of hours, or even overnight if you can spare the time.
7. To make the gnocchi, dust a chopping board with some extra coconut flour and slice the dough into equal sections. Roll each of those sections out on the coconut flour into a 1-inch rope, before cutting each rope into 1-inch pieces and set aside.
8. Once all the dough has been cut, use a gnocchi paddle or fork to create indentations in the gnocchi.
9. Next, bring a pot of water to a boil with a pinch of salt, before adding in the gnocchi in stages.
10. Let it cook for a couple minutes; once the gnocchi floats to the surface of the water, let it boil for 30 more seconds and then remove from the water using a slotted spoon. Continue this process until you have cooked all of the gnocchi.
11. The final step is where all of the flavour for this dish comes from! Heat a large pan (big enough to fit all of the gnocchi, or do this in two batches), add the butter and allow to melt. Once the butter is nice and hot add the sage leaves and allow to crisp on each side for about 30 secs.
12. Remove the sage and set aside before adding the garlic, lemon juice and zest followed by the pine nuts.
13. Toss in the gnocchi, season with salt and pepper and allow to brown for 2–3 minutes.
14. Serve and enjoy with the crispy sage leaves as your garnish.

VEGGIE BURGERS

Let me tell you, this recipe was a long time in the making. Veggie burgers are a difficult one to master in terms of getting the quantities correct. I'm pleased to announce that these are totally foolproof, super simple and packed full of flavour. Since their invention I've made countless batches – they're truly delicious and I hope you love them as much as I do. ☺

Makes 8–10 burgers

1 head of broccoli, separated into
    florets
1 large or 2 small sweet potatoes
    (~700g), peeled and diced
1 onion, finely chopped
1/2 cup milled flaxseeds
1 tsp garlic granules
2 tbsp Italian herb seasoning
Pinch of coarse sea salt
1 tsp olive oil (to grease the baking
    dish)

1. Preheat your oven to 200°C / 400°F.
2. In a large pot add the broccoli, sweet potato and onion, cover with water and bring to the boil before simmering for 20 minutes.
3. Strain off the water and add the veggies to a large bowl and mash until combined.
4. Mix in the remaining ingredients before separating out into patties.
5. Place on a greased baking dish and bake in the oven for 20 minutes, flipping for the last 5, until nice and crisp on the outside.
6. Serve and enjoy!

HARISSA ROASTED CHICKEN

A really delicious way of roasting a chicken with an added kick of flavour. A great one for a Sunday evening which yields plenty of leftovers for the week ahead.

Serves 4–6

1 large chicken
1 lemon
1/4 cup chicken stock
Pinch of coarse sea salt and cracked
    black pepper
2 tsp garlic and chilli oil (see p. 195)
1 tbsp mixed herbs
5–6 tbsp harissa paste

1. Preheat your oven to 200°C / 400°F.
2. Ensure the chicken is completely clean, remove any string and place on a board.
3. Zest the lemon, cut it in half and juice it. Add half the juice to a bowl with the zest, oil, herbs, and some salt and cracked black pepper.
4. Pour the remaining juice into the cavity of the chicken and place the squeezed lemon inside.
5. Rub the lemon and oil mixture over the chicken and sprinkle with a little more salt.
6. Place the chicken on a roasting tray and pour the stock around the chicken.
7. Roast in the oven for 20 minutes then reduce the heat to 180°C / 350°F and cook for a further 50–60 minutes until fully cooked.
8. Remove the chicken from the oven and coat it in the harissa paste before placing back in the oven on your grill setting for a further 10 minutes to caramelise and crisp up.
9. Serve and enjoy!

EASY SALMON TRAY BAKE

Salmon is one of my favourite things both to cook and to eat; it's a fantastic stand-alone staple that also works so well with so many different flavours.

This is a real pop-in-the-oven-and-let-it-do-the-hard-work recipe – perfect for those evenings when you just want to sit back, relax and wait for the cooker bell.

Serves 2

2 thick salmon darnes, skin on
400g sweet potato, skin on and cubed
Large handful of green beans, topped and tailed
1 carrot, peeled and diced
1 cup of broad beans
2 tbsp green pesto (see recipe p. 197)
2 tsp olive oil
2 cloves of garlic, minced
Coarse sea salt and cracked black pepper

1. Preheat your oven to 200°C / 400°F.
2. In a large ovenproof dish lay out the vegetables and toss in the olive oil and garlic with a sprinkle of coarse sea salt and pepper.
3. Bake in the oven for 15 minutes before removing and giving them a good toss.
4. Optional step: while the veggies are cooking, heat a large pan with some olive oil until smoking, season the salmon and place skin side down on the pan for 1–2 minutes until the skin is golden and crispy.
5. Place the salmon on top of the vegetables, brush with the pesto and bake in the oven for a further 10–12 minutes, until fully cooked to your liking.
6. Serve and enjoy!

PIRI-PIRI ZOODLES WITH CHICKEN AND PRAWNS

This is a brilliantly quick single-serve midweek meal. I make a variation of this at least once a week, if not more often.

Serves 1

1 large chicken breast, cut into strips
8–10 king prawns
200g (1/2 tin) chopped tomatoes
1 tbsp tomato purée
1/2 tsp piri-piri seasoning
1/2 tsp cumin
1/2 tsp paprika
1 tsp mixed herbs
1 clove of garlic, minced
2 tbsp lemon juice
Small knob of grassfed butter
1 courgette, sprialised
Large handful of spinach
Coarse sea salt
Olive oil

1. In a large pan heat the knob of butter and begin to cook the chicken and prawns with a sprinkle of coarse sea salt.
2. Add the tomato purée, herbs and spices along with the lemon juice and mix thoroughly.
3. Next add the chopped tomatoes and allow to heat through before reducing the heat and stirring in the spinach.
4. In another pan heat a teaspoon of olive oil and sauté the spiralised courgette for 3–4 minutes until cooked to your liking.
5. Serve and enjoy!

CAULIFLOWER MASALA

I love anything to do with cauliflower; it is one of my all-time favourite vegetables. This recipe is a great veggie alternative to an all-time classic.

Serves 2–3

1 large head of cauliflower
1/2 tsp mustard seeds
1 1/2 tsp ground turmeric
3 tsp garam masala
2 tsp ground coriander
1 tsp ground cinnamon
1 x 400g tin chopped tomatoes
1 x 142g tin tomato purée
250ml coconut cream
4 cloves of garlic, minced
1 jalapeño, finely chopped
1 red onion, finely sliced
1/2 inch ginger, grated
Olive oil
Pinch of coarse sea salt
Fresh coriander to serve

1. Preheat your oven to 200°C / 400°F and separate the cauliflower into florets.
2. Line a baking sheet with parchment and spread the cauliflower out, ensuring each piece has enough room.
3. Drizzle the oil over the cauliflower and toss until each piece is nicely coated, sprinkle some salt over the top and place in the oven.
4. Bake for 35–40 minutes, turning regularly, until golden and crispy.
5. In the meantime prepare the masala sauce: heat a large pot with some olive oil and sauté the onion, garlic, jalapeño and ginger.
6. In a dry pan, toast all of the spices for 1–2 minutes over a low heat.
7. Remove from the heat and place in a pestle and mortar; muddle until they are combined before adding to the pan with the onion mixture.
8. Cook for 1–2 minutes before stirring in the chopped tomatoes and purée followed by the coconut cream.
9. Bring the mixture to the boil and simmer for 10–15 minutes.
10. Once the cauliflower has finished cooking, stir it into the sauce.
11. Plate up and serve with a generous sprinkle of fresh coriander.

CHOCOLATE CHILLI CON CARNE

My mum has been making this recipe for as far back as I can remember; my version is true to the original with a little added twist – some chocolate! It really transforms the flavour and who doesn't love a little chocolate every now and then?

Serves 4–6

500g beef mince
1 tsp ground cumin
1/2 tsp hot chilli powder
Large pinch chipotle flakes
1 red onion, finely chopped
1 white onion, finely chopped
2 cloves of garlic, minced
1/2 red chilli, minced
1 x 400g tin of kidney beans
1 x 400g tin of tinned tomatoes
1 x 142g tin tomato purée
1/4 cup of vegetable stock
4 squares of dark chocolate
Olive / coconut oil
Coarse sea salt

1. Heat a large pot with some of your chosen oil and sauté the onions until they start to become translucent.
2. Add in the garlic, chilli and spices and cook until tender, adding a large pinch of salt.
3. Break up the mince and add to the pot, and brown for 6–8 minutes.
4. Next, add the chopped tomatoes, tomato purée and stock to the pan and heat for 2–3 minutes until it comes to a gentle boil.
5. Stir in the kidney beans before bringing the mixture back to the boil, reduce the heat and simmer for 15–20 minutes, until the mince is fully cooked and the sauce has thickened.
6. Lastly, add in the chocolate and stir through – serve and enjoy!

HAZEL AND NOEL'S AGE-OLD SPAG BOL

This is more than a recipe – it's a way of life. Every Saturday night for as far back as I can remember my parents have made a batch of this. Getting the recipe down on ink was a tricky one – but here it is and we hope you love it as much as we do!

Serves 8–10

3lbs round steak mince
2 onions, diced
6 stalks of celery, finely chopped
1 large packet of bacon lardons
500g mushrooms, quartered
2 x 142g tins tomato purée
3 x 400g tins chopped tomatoes
650ml tomato passata
3 bay leaves, cracked
4 cloves of garlic, minced
2 tbsp Italian herbs
1 tbsp oregano
1 tbsp nutmeg
1–2 tbsp honey
1/2 pint beef stock
2 glasses of good quality red wine
Coarse sea salt and cracked black
   pepper
Olive oil

1. Begin with a large pot. Add the chopped tomatoes, tomato purée, passata and honey along with the stock and place over a gentle heat.
2. Heat a large pan with some olive oil and fry the bacon lardons for 2–3 minutes before adding the celery and onion.
3. Allow the celery and onion to cook down for 2–3 minutes before adding the garlic, Italian herbs, oregano, bay leaves and nutmeg. Cook for a further 2–3 minutes before transferring the mixture to the pot with the sauce.
4. Add another small bit of olive oil to the pan if needed and begin to brown the mince in 2 batches with some salt and pepper. Once it has started to brown add 1 glass of wine (per batch) and cook for a further 2 minutes before placing into the pot with the sauce.
5. At this point add the mushrooms to the pot and give everything a thorough stir. Turn up the heat and bring the mixture to the boil before reducing to a simmer for 25–30 minutes.
6. Serve and enjoy with either zoodles or pasta.

CREAMY SALMON SKILLET

This is the perfect indulgent dish for a Friday night in. Why not have the second half-glass of wine as you make it?

Serves 2

2 salmon darnes
1 tsp olive oil
1 tbsp grassfed butter
3 cloves of garlic, minced
1 onion, diced
1/2 glass of white wine
130g sundried tomatoes
1 cup (250ml) coconut cream
2 large handfuls of spinach
1 tsp arrowroot powder
Fresh parsley, to garnish

1. Heat a large pan with some olive oil and fry the salmon for 2–3 minutes per side before removing from the pan and setting aside.
2. Add the butter to the pan and allow to melt; add the garlic and onion and sauté for 1–2 minutes before adding the wine.
3. Add the tomatoes and cook for a further minute before adding the coconut cream.
4. Give the mixture a stir and bring to the boil before reducing to a gentle simmer for roughly 2 minutes until everything is heated through, then stir in the spinach and allow to wilt.
5. Finally, thicken the sauce with the arrowroot powder before adding the salmon back into the pan.
6. Once the salmon is heated through and fully cooked, serve and enjoy with some freshly chopped parsley scattered on top.

THE ULTIMATE WEEKEND INDULGENCE

CHICKEN WINGS 3 WAYS

I adore chicken wings – if you've followed my blog for any length of time you'll likely know this already. The possibilities are endless when it comes to cooking methods, marinades and flavour combos. It was tough but these three are definitely amongst my favourites – I hope you love them!

Serves 4–6

Hot and Sticky Wannngs
900g chicken wings
1/4 cup Frank's Red Hot Sauce
1/4 cup honey
2 heaped tbsp wholegrain mustard

1. In a large bowl combine hot sauce, mustard and honey.
2. Add the wings to the bowl and cover in the mixture.
3. Preheat the oven to 220°C / 428°F, place the wings on a baking tray skin side up and bake for 8 minutes before flipping over and cooking for a further 8 minutes.
4. Remove from the oven, flip back over to skin side up and brush with any remaining marinate before baking for a further 6–8 minutes until crispy, serve and enjoy!

Lemon Pepper
900g chicken wings
4 tbsp cayenne pepper
Juice and zest of 2 large lemons
20g grassfed butter
1 tbsp cracked black pepper
2 tbsp flat-leaved parsley – finely chopped
Lemon wedges to serve

1. Preheat your oven to 220°C / 428°F.
2. Place the chicken wings on a wire rack and rub the cayenne pepper into the skin.
3. Bake in the oven for 8 minutes, then turn them over and return them to the oven for a further 8 minutes.
4. Melt the butter and mix it with the lemon juice. Remove the wings from the oven and cover with the lemon and butter mix, return to the oven skin side up for a further 10 minutes, or until golden and crispy.
5. Place the wings in a large bowl and toss with the zest, cracked black pepper and parsley. Serve and enjoy!

Asian-Style
900g chicken wings
4 spring onions
1 tbsp coconut aminos
1/2 tsp dried thyme
1/2 tsp dried sage
1/2 tsp 5 spice powder
1 tbsp white wine vinegar
1 red chilli, chopped
4 cloves of garlic, peeled and chopped
1 inch fresh ginger, peeled and chopped
2 bay leaves

1. Preheat your oven to 220°C / 428°F.
2. Roughly chop the spring onions, put all the ingredients in the food processor and blend until liquidised.
3. In a large bowl combine the chicken wings and the marinade.
4. Place in a large ziplock or airtight bag and leave in the fridge to marinade for as long as possible.
5. Place the wings on a wire rack and bake in the oven for 15–20 minutes, turning regularly until they are cooked through and the skin is nice and crispy. Serve and enjoy!

SESAME CHICKEN THIGHS

This is a really delicious one-tray wonder – packed full of nutrients yet maintains that little feeling of decadence with its amazing flavour! If you have some time to spare leave the chicken to marinade in the sauce for a couple of hours or even overnight. It will be all the more delicious!

Serves 4

5 chicken thighs, bone in, skin on
1 head of broccoli, separated into florets
1 head pak choi, chopped
2 tbsp sesame seeds

For the sauce:
3 cloves of garlic, minced
6 spring onions, finely chopped
1 tbsp grated ginger
1 tsp 5 spice powder (optional)
1 tbsp sesame oil
2 tbsp honey
4 tbsp coconut aminos
1 green chilli, finely chopped
Coarse sea salt and cracked black pepper
Olive oil

1. Preheat your oven to 200°C / 400°F.
2. In your food processor combine all of the sauce ingredients along with a good pinch of coarse sea salt, until you have a runny paste.
3. Add the sauce and the chicken thighs to a large bowl and mix thoroughly until the chicken is fully coated in the sauce.
4. Toss the broccoli and pak choi in some olive oil, sprinkle with salt and pepper and set aside.
5. Lay the chicken out onto a baking dish and sprinkle over the sesame seeds.
6. Bake in the oven for 20 minutes before adding the broccoli and pak choi and cooking for a further 15–20 minutes until the veggies are nice and crispy and the chicken is cooked through. Serve and enjoy!

CHICKEN KATSU

This is such a crowd pleaser and total comfort food – I love to serve mine with some cauliflower rice and roasted green beans on the side but it's totally up to you and what you're in the mood for.

Serves 2

2 chicken breast fillets, butterflied
Sprinkle coconut flour
1 egg, beaten
100g ground almonds
Olive oil
Coarse sea salt and cracked black
   pepper

For the curry sauce:
4 shallots, diced
1/2 chilli, finely chopped
2 carrots, peeled and chopped
3 cloves of garlic, minced
2 tbsp curry powder
500ml chicken stock
2 tbsp honey
2 tbsp coconut aminos
1 tsp cumin
1 tsp turmeric
1 bay leaf
1 tsp garam masala

Spring onions, finely chopped to serve
Sprinkle of sesame seeds

1. Preheat your oven to 200°C / 400°F.
2. Begin by making the curry sauce: heat a saucepan with some oil, add the shallots, chilli and garlic and cook until softened. Add the carrots and cook over a low heat for 6–8 minutes until they start to soften.
3. Stir in the curry powder and spices before cooking for a further minute. Gradually stir in the chicken stock until combined.
4. Next, add all of the remaining ingredients for the sauce and bring the mixture to the boil.
5. Reduce the heat and simmer for 15–20 minutes until sauce thickens.
6. Finally blend into a sauce, adding some additional chicken stock to loosen it up if needed.
7. To make the chicken, season both sides of the chicken breasts with salt and pepper.
8. Coat the chicken breasts in the coconut flour, then dip into the egg, before covering in the ground almonds.
9. Heat some oil in a large frying pan over a medium-high heat. Place the chicken into the pan and cook until golden brown, about 1–2 minutes each side.
10. Place the chicken on a baking dish and bake in the oven for 10 minutes, until fully cooked through.
11. Remove the chicken from the oven, slice and lay on some cauliflower rice, pour the curry sauce over the chicken and garnish with some spring onions and sesame seeds. Serve and enjoy!

FRIED 'RICE'

I have such lovely memories of my mum making homemade fried rice as a treat when we were small. Switching up the original recipe with cauliflower is a great way to get extra veggies in!

Serves 2–3

1 large head of cauliflower, blitzed into small chunks
2 large eggs, beaten
200g frozen peas
2 carrots, finely diced
3 cloves of garlic, minced
3 spring onions, finely sliced
1/2 tsp fish sauce
6 tbsp coconut aminos
Your chosen oil
Coarse sea salt and cracked black pepper
Fresh parsley, chopped, to garnish

1. Begin by heating a large pan or wok with a small amount of oil.
2. Add the eggs and cook for 1–2 minutes until solid and in the form of a really thin omelette, flip over and cook on the other side for another minute before removing from the pan and setting aside.
3. Next sauté the cauliflower for 10–12 minutes until it starts to soften.
4. Add in the remainder of the veggies with a splash of water and cook for a further 5–10 minutes until everything is nicely cooked through.
5. Add the fish sauce and coconut aminos and stir through with some seasoning.
6. Slice up the egg and add to the wok before serving. Sprinkle over the parsley, serve and enjoy!

MONGOLIAN BEEF

A play on a recipe from one of my favourite Asian restaurants – using ribeye steak.

This is a great little one for a quick and easy Friday night in; the steak can be subbed for any cut of meat you have to hand but if you can I really recommend trying it with ribeye – it's drool-worthy!

Serves 2

2 ribeye steaks, cut into strips
1 red onion, finely sliced
2 peppers, finely sliced
Large handful of mushrooms, finely
    sliced
4 spring onions, finely sliced
Olive oil
Coarse sea salt and cracked black
    pepper

For the sauce:
2 tsp arrowroot powder
1 tsp sesame oil
4 cloves of garlic, minced
2 inches of ginger, grated
2 chillies, finely sliced
1 cup of coconut aminos
2 tbsp honey

1. Heat a large pan with some olive oil and sear the steak with a good pinch of coarse sea salt for 1–2 minutes per side before setting aside.
2. In the meantime, add all of the sauce ingredients to a small pot, bring to the boil and allow to simmer while you prepare the rest of the dish.
3. Heat a large pan or wok with some olive oil and lightly sauté the onion, peppers and spring onions for 4–5 minutes until they start to soften.
4. Add the mushrooms and cook the veggies for a further 2–3 minutes before adding in the sauce.
5. Finally, add the steak to the pan and cook for a further couple of minutes until it is cooked to your liking. Serve and enjoy!

CHICKEN AND BROCCOLI STIR FRY

The perfect meal in a minute for one, for nights when it's just you but you're feeling a little fancy.

Serves 1

180g broccoli, separated into florets
60g red onion, finely sliced
1 large chicken breast, sliced into strips
2 cloves of garlic, minced
1/4 red chilli, finely chopped
1/8 tsp ginger powder
4 tbsp coconut aminos
1 tbsp honey
1 tbsp sesame oil
Pinch of coarse sea salt

1. Heat a large wok or frying pan with the sesame oil.
2. Add the onion and sauté for 1–2 minutes before adding the garlic and chilli, along with a pinch of coarse sea salt, and sautéing for a further 2 minutes.
3. In the meantime, steam the broccoli for 2 minutes.
4. Add the chicken to the wok and allow to brown.
5. Next, add the broccoli to the wok and cook everything together for 2–3 minutes.
6. Lastly add the coconut aminos and honey, stir until all of the ingredients are nicely coated.
7. Reduce the heat and leave to simmer for 2–3 minutes.
8. Once the chicken is fully cooked, serve and enjoy.

SWEET POTATO CHILLI FRIES

An assembly process more so than anything – these chilli fries are perfect for a Friday night in!

Serves 3–4

1–2 portions of leftover chilli con carne
   (see recipe on p. 127)
2 large sweet potatoes
2 tsp garlic and chilli oil (see p. 195)
1 tsp cayenne powder
1/2 tsp smoked paprika
Large pinch of coarse sea salt
Large handful of chopped coriander
   to garnish

1. Preheat your oven to 200°C / 400°F.
2. Slice the sweet potato into fries, leaving the skin on.
3. In a large bowl, add the oil and spices, sprinkle with some salt and stir until combined.
4. Add the sweet potato to the bowl and toss until coated in the oil mixture.
5. Lay the fries out on a baking tray lined with baking parchment and place in the oven.
6. Bake in the oven for 40–45 minutes until crispy and cooked to your liking.
7. In the meantime heat the chilli in a small pot. Once fully heated through, spoon on top of the fries, sprinkle with some coriander and enjoy!

STICKY BBQ RIBS

I adore BBQ season and these ribs are outrageously tasty – if you have your barbeque fired up and ready to go, skip the grilling at the end and pop them straight on the barbie!

Serves 10–12

12 large pork ribs
Coarse sea salt and cracked black
  pepper

For the sauce:
1 portion of my sticky BBQ sauce (see
  p. 203)

1. Season the ribs and marinade in half of the BBQ sauce for a couple of hours (overnight if you can spare the time).
2. To begin the cooking process, preheat your oven to 160°C / 320°F.
3. Place the ribs on baking tray, cover with tinfoil and bake in the oven for 4–5 hours until tender.
4. Once the ribs are fully cooked and tender remove from the oven and move to an ovenproof dish with a wire rack.
5. Using a pastry brush, baste the ribs with some additional BBQ sauce before placing under the grill for 1–2 minutes per side, until slightly crispy.
6. Serve with the remaining BBQ sauce and enjoy with your choice of side dishes.

BBQ PULLED PORK

Pulled pork is such an easy thing to prepare – let the oven do all of the hard work and swoop in at the end to shred and get the glory. Enjoy!

Serves 6–8

2.5kg pork shoulder
4 tbsp olive oil
4 cloves of garlic, minced
1/2 chilli, finely chopped
3 tbsp red wine vinegar
2 tsp smoked paprika
Coarse sea salt and cracked black
    pepper

For the sauce:
1 x 400g tin of chopped tomatoes
2 tbsp tomato purée
1/4 cup apple cider vinegar
2 tsp garlic granules
1 tsp smoked paprika
3 tbsp molasses
Pinch of chipotle flakes
Coarse sea salt and cracked black
    pepper

1. Preheat your oven to 160°C / 320°F.
2. In a small bowl combine all of the marinade ingredients and rub it into the pork shoulder.
3. Place the pork on a baking tray and bake in the oven for 4 hours, until tender.
4. In the meantime place all of the sauce ingredients in a small pot and whisk to combine.
5. Place over a medium-high heat and bring to the boil before reducing to a simmer for 15 minutes.
6. Remove the sauce from the heat and set aside while the pork cooks away.
7. Once the pork is fully cooked and tender remove from the oven and allow to cool slightly before shredding.
8. Once fully shredded toss in the BBQ sauce and serve with your choice of sides.
   My favourite way to serve this is with some cos lettuce and chopped up veggies, like cucumber and radish.

SIDES

HOMEMADE TATER TOTS

A super-simple version of one of my all-time favourites. There are tonnes more variations of these on my website so don't be shy – once you master this recipe head over and check them out.

Serves 3–4

1kg sweet potatoes
1 tbsp garlic and chilli oil (see p. 195)
4 shallots, finely diced
1 egg
Coarse sea salt and cracked black
    pepper
2 tsp coconut oil

1. Preheat your oven to 200°C / 400°F.
2. Peel the sweet potato and cut into chunks, toss in the olive oil. Bake in the oven until tender, approximately 15–20 minutes depending on the thickness of your chunks.
3. In a large bowl mash the sweet potato, add the shallots and egg, season and mix thoroughly.
4. Use your hands to squeeze and shape the mixture into 'tots'.
5. Lay them out on a baking sheet lined with parchment paper.
6. Bake for 10 minutes, drizzle a little coconut oil over the tots and bake for a further 10 minutes before turning.
7. Bake on the opposite side for a further 5–10 minutes, until golden and crispy, serve with some homemade mayo for dipping and enjoy!

FOOL-PROOF SWEET POTATO FRIES

Everyone needs this recipe in their repertoire – it's a good one.

Serves 2

400g sweet potato, skin on, cut into
   fries
2 tsp olive or coconut oil
1 tsp garlic granules
1 tsp Italian herb seasoning
Coarse sea salt and cracked black
   pepper

1. Preheat your oven to 210°C / 410°F.
2. Toss the fries in your chosen oil and the seasoning before laying out on a parchment-lined baking tray.
3. Bake in the oven for 20–25 minutes, tossing after 15 minutes.
4. Serve and enjoy – you can thank me later for sharing the tricks of the trade. ☺

HASSELBACK BABY POTATOES

For years I shied away from white potatoes and boy was I missing out! Baby potatoes are my favourite by a mile; they're so delicious, especially when you do them as hasselbacks.

Serves 3–4

1 kg baby potatoes
4 cloves of garlic, crushed
4 sprigs of rosemary, leaves separated
   from the stalk
2 tbsp olive oil
2 tbsp grassfed butter
Coarse sea salt and cracked black
   pepper

1. Preheat your oven to 200°C / 400°F.
2. Working from one end of the potato to the other make thin slices three-quarters of the way through the potatoes a few millimetres apart.
3. Place the potatoes on a baking tray. Mix the oil, garlic and rosemary together with some coarse sea salt and cracked black pepper before patting onto the potatoes; ensure that some of the oil is on the bottom to stop them from sticking.
4. Bake in the oven for 30–35 minutes until golden and crispy, basting halfway through with the butter. Serve and enjoy!

PARSNIP FRIES

Oftentimes parsnips can get a bad rep, but in actual fact they are such a great root vegetable and really versatile. My cottage pie on page 111 is testament to this! I adore making fries out of them too and I have a feeling you are going to love these. ☺

Serves 2

4 parsnips
2 tbsp olive oil
1 tsp garam masala
1 tsp cumin
Coarse sea salt and cracked black
    pepper

1. Preheat your oven to 200°C / 400°F.
2. Scrub the parsnips and slice into chips, leaving the skin on.
3. In a large bowl combine the olive oil, spices, salt and pepper.
4. Toss the parsnip chips in the oil mixture before laying out on a baking tray in a single layer.
5. Bake in the oven for 20–25 minutes until golden and crispy, tossing midway through.

BAKED CAULIFLOWER WITH RAISINS AND PINE NUTS

The inspiration for this recipe came from eating a similar dish out – I couldn't wait to get home to try it out myself and put my own spin on it. If you haven't figured it out already I love cauliflower and get very excited about it!

Serves 2–4

1 large head of cauliflower, separated
  into florets
3–4 tbsp olive oil
3 tbsp pine nuts
5 tbsp raisins
Zest and juice of 1/2 lemon
Coarse sea salt and cracked black pepper
Large handful of chopped coriander
  to serve

1. Preheat your oven to 200°C / 400°F.
2. In a large bowl combine the cauliflower, lemon juice, zest, salt and pepper.
3. Lay out on a baking tray and place in the oven for 30 minutes, tossing halfway through.
4. Remove from the oven and scatter the raisins and pine nuts onto the tray, tossing the cauliflower one more time. Bake in the oven for a further 10 minutes.
5. Serve with a generous handful of chopped coriander.

SWEET POTATO CROQUETTES

I am a huge fan of tapas, particularly croquettes. Believe it or not, these bad boys were one of my first ever creations way back at the beginning of The Wonky Spatula – I'd been holding them back for a special occasion and now seems like the perfect time to share. Hope you love them as much as I do!

Serves 6

500g sweet potato
200g bacon lardons
1 tbsp olive oil (or check out my garlic
    and chilli oil on p. 195)
1 red onion, finely diced
1/4 pepper, diced
1/4 cup ground almonds
2 tsp coconut flour
1 egg
1 tsp coconut oil
Coarse sea salt and cracked black
    pepper

1. Toss the sweet potato in the garlic and chilli oil and season with salt and pepper. Bake at 220°C / 428°F for 15 minutes, until cooked through but not too crisped on the outside.
2. Fry off the lardons in a large pan with some coconut oil; allow to crisp before removing from the heat and setting aside.
3. Place the sweet potato in a large bowl and allow to cool slightly before mashing.
4. Add the onions, pepper and lardons to the sweet potato and combine.
5. Using your hands, split the mixture in six pieces and roll into croquettes, dusting the outside of each with some coconut flour.
6. Beat the egg in a small bowl and lay the ground almonds out on a flat plate.
7. Individually coat the croquettes in the egg before rolling in the ground almonds.
8. Heat the pan that was used to cook the lardons, adding more coconut oil to the bacon fat if necessary, and brown the croquettes over a medium heat for roughly 1 minute each side. Serve and enjoy!

THE BEST EVER CARROTS

Honestly, when these came out of the oven for the first time I dipped one in the sauce, tasted it and then started doing a happy dance around the kitchen – fast forward to 5 minutes later and there wasn't a carrot or a drop of sauce in sight – they're *that* good!

Serves 3–4

750g baby carrots, whole
2 tbsp olive oil
1/2 tsp garam masala
1/2 tsp curry powder
2 cloves of garlic, minced
Coarse sea salt and cracked black
    pepper

For the dip:
3 tbsp honey
3 tbsp coconut aminos
2 tbsp almond butter
1/8 tsp garlic granules
Coarse sea salt and cracked black
    pepper

Handful of fresh coriander to serve

1. Preheat your oven to 200°C / 400°F.
2. Lay the carrots out on a baking tray and toss in the oil and spices before seasoning.
3. Bake in the oven for 1 hour, tossing every 15–20 minutes.
4. To make the dip, simply combine everything in a small bowl and set aside until the carrots are fully cooked.
5. Remove the carrots from the oven, drizzle over the sauce and sprinkle with some fresh coriander, serve and enjoy!

CRACK CAULIFLOWER

Cauliflower is one of the best vegetables out there – it's so versatile as you will hopefully have seen with the amount of times it rears its head in this book. This crack cauliflower takes it to the next level – you won't be able to get enough!

Serves 3–4

1 head cauliflower, separated into
    florets
2 large eggs, beaten
1/2 cup ground almonds
1/2 cup coconut flour
1/4 cup arrowroot powder
Pinch cayenne pepper
Coarse sea salt and cracked black
    pepper
Olive oil

For the sauce:
1/2 cup sticky BBQ sauce (see p. 203)
1/4 cup honey or maple syrup
1 clove of garlic, minced
Pinch of chilli flakes
1/4 tsp smoked paprika
Juice of 1 lime

1. Preheat your oven to 200°C / 400°F.
2. In a large bowl combine the almonds, coconut flour, arrowroot powder, salt, pepper and cayenne pepper.
3. In another bowl add the eggs.
4. Dip each floret in the egg and then roll it in the flour mixture. Repeat until all florets are covered.
5. Heat a large pan with some olive oil and cook the cauliflower in batches for ~1 minute a side until crispy and golden.
6. Once the cauliflower is nicely golden place on a baking tray and bake in the oven for 20 minutes.
7. In the meantime, prepare the sauce by heating all of the ingredients over a low heat and setting aside until the cauliflower is fully cooked.
8. Serve and enjoy!

BAKED SPROUTS

If you have followed my blog you will most likely already know that I am a huge fan of sprouts. I really just can't get enough of them. This recipe is super simple and shows them off just perfectly!

Serves 2

320g sprouts, halved
1 packet of bacon lardons
1 tbsp olive oil
Coarse sea salt and cracked black
    pepper

1. Preheat your oven to 200°C / 400°F.
2. On a large baking tray lay out the sprouts and bacon, toss in olive oil and sprinkle with salt and pepper.
3. Bake in the oven for 25–30 minutes, tossing halfway through.
4. Serve and enjoy!

BOG STANDARD BAKED VEGGIES

Baked veggies are the perfect thing to have cooked in advance for the week ahead. It's also a great way to revitalise any vegetables that may have started to look a bit sad in the fridge by the end of the week.

Serves 4–6

3 peppers, diced
5 cloves of garlic, minced
1 leek, diced
1 head of broccoli, separated into
    florets
4 carrots, peeled and sliced
4 stalks of celery, roughly chopped
2–3 tbsp of olive oil
Pinch of chipotle flakes
Coarse sea salt and cracked black
    pepper

1. Preheat your oven to 200°C / 400°F.
2. Lay out the veggies on a large baking dish, toss in the olive oil and sprinkle with salt, pepper and chipotle flakes.
3. Bake in the oven for 45–50 minutes, tossing occasionally – it really couldn't be any easier!

RAINBOW VEGGIE TRAY BAKE

For those weeks when you're feeling a little bit fancy with your meal prep!

Serves 3–4

200g baby aubergines
250g rainbow carrots
300g baby parsnips
1 green pepper
1 tsp garam masala
1 tsp oregano
1 tsp dried parsley
Coarse sea salt and cracked black
    pepper
2 tbsp olive oil

1. Preheat your oven to 200°C / 400°F.
2. Prepare the vegetables by halving the aubergines, carrots and parsnips, and slicing the pepper into thin strips.
3. Lay out the veggies on a large baking dish, toss in the olive oil and sprinkle with the seasoning, salt and pepper. Give everything a good toss to ensure all of the veggies are evenly coated.
4. Bake in the oven for 40–45 minutes, tossing occasionally.
5. Serve and enjoy.

TOP BLOG POSTS

SWEET POTATO DISC STACKS

I have been in love with this recipe since day one; it's such a crowd pleaser and super simple to make.

I've been making this for over six years now and I never grow tired of it. It's a great one to have up your sleeve for weekend brunches. Take it to the next level of luxury with some sautéed greens and poached eggs.

Serves 2

1 sweet potato, peeled
1 tbsp dried oregano
6–8 slices streaky bacon
2 tbsp of coconut oil

1. Preheat the oven to 220°C / 428°F.
2. Cut the sweet potato into discs.
3. Melt 1 tbsp of coconut oil and toss the sweet potato in it.
4. Place the discs on a baking tray and sprinkle with oregano on both sides.
5. Bake in the oven for 10–15 minutes, turning halfway.
6. Remove the potatoes from the oven and wrap them in bacon.
7. Heat a small amount of coconut oil in a pan and fry the discs for 2–3 minutes a side, until the bacon is fully cooked and crispy.
8. Plate up and enjoy! These can be spiced up with a bit of cayenne pepper if you're feeling adventurous – just sprinkle it on with/instead of the oregano.

CLEAN BONELESS BITES

Without a shadow of a doubt this has been the most popular recipe on my blog since day one. Once you try it you'll be making it for life – trust me!

Serves 3–4

2–3 large chicken breasts
1 egg, beaten
1/4 cup ground almonds
2 tbsp coconut flour
1/4 cup Frank's Red Hot Sauce
1 tbsp grassfed butter
4 stalks of celery
Coarse sea salt and cracked black
    pepper

1. Preheat the oven to 220°C / 428°F.
2. Chop the chicken breasts up into bite-sized pieces.
3. Place the pieces in a bowl with the beaten egg.
4. Mix the ground almonds and coconut flour together, season and lay out on a large dinner plate.
5. One by one, cover the chicken breast in egg and then roll it in the flour until coated.
6. Repeat until all of the chicken is covered.
7. Place the chicken on a wire rack and bake in the oven until golden brown and cooked through – roughly 8 minutes a side.
8. In a small saucepan heat the hot sauce and butter for 2–3 minutes, then add to a large bowl.
9. Once the chicken has finished cooking, remove from the oven and add to the bowl with the hot sauce.
10. Toss the bites in the sauce.
11. Plate up and serve with celery sticks and any leftover hot sauce for dipping. Enjoy!

THE WONKY CURRY

The Wonky Curry is the perfect mix between a rich nutty flavour and gorgeous spice; it was the happy by-product of a kitchen disaster and after some adjustments were made it made its way to the blog where it is enjoyed on a weekly basis by readers.

Serves 4

3 large chicken breasts, cut into chunks
1 large white onion, finely sliced
2 bell peppers, finely sliced
1 thumb-sized piece of ginger, grated
3 cloves of garlic, minced
1 red chilli, finely sliced
150g button mushrooms, thinly sliced
1/2 tbsp ground turmeric
1/2 tbsp medium curry powder
1/2 tbsp garam masala
1 can of coconut milk
3 heaped tbsp crunchy almond butter
Coconut oil

1. In a large wok heat 1 tbsp of coconut oil and sauté the chicken for 4–6 minutes until lightly browned.
2. Remove the chicken and set aside. Add a little more oil to the pan and sauté the onions.
3. After about 1–2 minutes, when the onions have started to become translucent, add in the garlic, chilli, ginger, turmeric, garma masala and curry powder. Mix thoroughly, adding a teaspoon or so of water if necessary.
4. Allow the onions and spices to cook for 2–3 minutes before adding in the peppers and mushrooms.
5. Once the peppers have started to soften add the chicken back into the wok, followed by the almond butter.
6. Give everything a good stir and add in the coconut milk, stirring again until it has fully combined.
7. Allow the mixture to come to a gentle boil (you want it to start to bubble slightly around the edges) before reducing the heat and simmering for 8–10 minutes, stirring occasionally, until the chicken is fully cooked and the sauce is rich and creamy.
8. Serve and enjoy!

THE WONKY VEG CURRY

A natural progression from the original Wonky Curry. This dish is packed full of flavour and so nutritious. It's perfect as a meal by itself and also incredible with some spinach stirred through at the end for an extra boost of goodness and a side of cauliflower rice.

Serves 4

2 red onions, finely sliced
2 bell peppers, finely sliced
2 cloves of garlic, minced
1/2 red chilli, finely sliced
1 tbsp ground turmeric
2 tbsp curry powder
1 tbsp garam masala
1 tbsp ground cumin
1 aubergine, cubed
2 small or 1 large sweet potato, peeled
   and cubed
1/2 head of cauliflower, separated into
   florets
1 x 400g can of coconut milk
1/4 cup crunchy almond butter
Coconut oil

1. In a large wok heat 1 tbsp of coconut oil and sauté the onions for 2–3 minutes.
2. Add in the spices and mix until the onions are nice and coated, then add in 1/4 cup of water to create the curry paste.
3. After about 1–2 minutes, when the onions have started to become translucent, add in the garlic and chilli.
4. Allow the onions and spices to cook for 2–3 minutes before adding the aubergine.
5. Once the aubergine has started to soften add in the rest of the vegetables and mix thoroughly.
6. Give everything a good stir and add in the coconut milk, stirring again until it has fully combined, followed by the almond butter.
7. Allow the mixture to come to a gentle boil (you want it to start to bubble slightly around the edges) before reducing the heat and simmering for 8–10 minutes, stirring occasionally, until the vegetables are nice and soft and the sauce is rich and creamy.
8. Serve and enjoy!

BANOFFEE PIE

Just like all of the recipes in this section, my banoffee pie has been around for a long time! I absolutely adore banoffee – this recipe is the perfect healthier alternative to a traditional family favourite.

Serves 8–10

2 x 400g tins of full fat coconut milk
   refrigerated for 6–8 hours
400g raw cashew nuts
1 tbsp melted coconut oil
1 tbsp solid coconut oil
6–8 pecans
2 cups of dates
1/4 cup + 1 tbsp of agave syrup
1/2 tsp ground cinnamon
1 square of 85% dark chocolate
2–3 ripe bananas

1. Preheat your oven to 200°C / 400°F.
2. Place the cashews on a baking tray and toast for 6–8 minutes, until they begin to go golden brown.
3. Soak the dates in hot water and set aside to soften.
4. Place the cashews in the food processor and blend until you have a flour-like mixture.
5. Add 1 tbsp of melted coconut oil and 1/4 cup of agave syrup to the cashew flour and blend until the mixture is combined.
6. Line an 8″ cake tin with parchment.
7. Add the mixture to the tin and smooth out with a flat spoon or small rolling pin; place in the fridge while you prepare the caramel.
8. Remove the stones from the dates and add to the food processor along with about 100mls of the water they were soaking in.
9. Blend until the mixture looks like a smooth caramel, then add the cinnamon, 1 tbsp of solid coconut oil and 1 tbsp of agave syrup and blend again. When all the ingredients have combined, add the pecans and blend until smooth.
10. Remove the base from the fridge and add the caramel; refrigerate for 1–2 hours or until set.
11. Carefully remove the coconut milk from the fridge and open the cans. The milk should have solidified at the top – scoop out the thick 'cream' and discard the water from the bottom.
12. Whip the coconut cream until ripples begin to appear on the surface.
13. Remove the base from the fridge and layer the caramel with slices of banana.
14. Transfer the pie onto a serving plate and smooth the cream over the banana.
15. Grate the chocolate and sprinkle it on top.

SAUCES, DIPS AND SPREADS

MUM'S BBQ SAUCE

My mum has made endless batches of this sauce every summer for as long as I can remember. It is insanely delicious and can go on absolutely everything! Believe me I've tried, from traditional BBQ dinners to baked eggs, it is the ultimate summer staple.

1 tbsp olive oil
2 cloves of garlic, crushed
1 white onion, finely diced
1 x 400g tin chopped tomatoes
1 x 142g tin tomato purée
3 tbsp honey
2 tbsp of red wine vinegar
1 tsp chilli powder
1 tsp mustard

1. In a large sauce pan add the oil and allow to heat. Sweat down the onions with the garlic for 3–5 minutes until soft.
2. Add the rest of the ingredients, bring to the boil and simmer for roughly 15 minutes until thickened.
3. It really is that simple – allow to cool and keep in the fridge for up to a week, if it lasts that long!

THE ULTIMATE GUACAMOLE

I absolutely love homemade guacamole. It is so delicious and super simple to make. A total fridge staple if you ask me. The key here really is the avocados so make sure they're super ripe.

2–3 ripe avocados
Small handful of coriander, roughly
    chopped
Juice of 1 lime
2 cloves of garlic, minced
1/2 jalapeno, finely chopped
1/4 tsp chipotle flakes
1/4 tsp smoked paprika
1 tomato, finely diced
1/2 red onion, finely diced
Sprinkle of cracked black pepper and
    coarse sea salt

1. Mince the avocados with a fork until smooth.
2. Add them to a bowl with the rest of the ingredients and mix until combined.
3. Serve and enjoy – it really is that simple!

GRILLED PEPPERS

Grilled peppers are one of my favourite things to have prepped in the fridge. They're great in salads, as burger toppings, or just to munch on by themselves.

As many peppers as you have on hand

1. Take the peppers, cut them in quarters and remove the seeds.
2. Place on a wire rack, skin side up, and grill on high until the skin has gone completely black.
3. Remove from the oven and place in a ziplock bag, leaving it sealed until the peppers are completely cooled.
4. Once they have cooled remove from the bag and skin them.
5. Cut into thin strips and place in a jar, seal and refrigerate.
6. The longer you leave them to set before eating them the better, as a natural oil develops, making them all the more flavoursome.

NICOLA'S TIP

This is a really super recipe to use up any peppers you have on hand that have lost their crunch; think of it as a rescue recipe.

GARLIC AND CHILLI OIL

I use this oil for absolutely everything; it's great for adding flavour and making a seemly boring dinner that little bit more exciting. Anytime I have some chillies that are starting to go a bit shrivelled I whip up a batch. It's a total store cupboard staple for a tonne of recipes in this book.

1 cup of extra virgin olive oil
3–4 cloves of garlic, crushed
2 chillies, finely chopped with the
    seeds removed

1. Combine all of the ingredients.
2. If you are not using it straight away leave to mature for 2–3 days; if you're under pressure for time put it over a medium to low heat for 1–2 minutes until it has infused.
3. Store in a sterilized container.

HUMMUS

A basic but essential recipe to have up your sleeve. If you have the time/patience, I really recommend peeling the skin off the chickpeas before you begin, it makes it so incredibly creamy!

1 x 400g tin of chickpeas
2 cloves of garlic, minced
Juice of 1 lemon
1/2 cup of chickpea water, from the tin
2 tbsp olive oil
Sprinkle of coarse sea salt
1/2 tsp smoked paprika
1/2 tsp ground cumin
1/2 cup of dark tahini

1. Add the chickpeas, lemon juice, chickpea water, garlic, oil, a good pinch of sea salt, paprika and cumin to your food processor.
2. Blend on high for 2–3 minutes until completely smooth.
3. Add in the tahini and blend on high again until mixed through and smooth.
4. Add to a bowl, sprinkle with some more smoked paprika and enjoy.

PESTO

A great homemade version in place of store-bought pesto to have on hand – feel free to make a double batch!

50g pine nuts
50g cashews
100ml olive oil
2 bunches of basil or parsley
2 cloves of garlic
2 tbsp lemon juice

1. In a large dry pan toast the pine nuts and cashews for 2–3 minutes until golden.
2. Place all of the ingredients bar the oil in your food processor and blend until smooth.
3. Run your food processor on low and slowly pour in the olive oil until it is all in and the pesto is lovely and smooth.

CHIA JAM

The easiest jam on the planet – FACT!

250g raspberries
2 tbsp of chia seeds
2 tbsp of agave
1 tsp of vanilla extract

1. Rinse the raspberries in some cold water and strain them off, leaving a small bit of water on them.
2. Place in a saucepan over a low heat for 5–10 minutes until they start to soften, stirring regularly.
3. Stir in the chia seeds and cook for a further minute or so before finally stirring in the agave and the vanilla.
4. Remove from the heat and allow to cool slightly before placing into a sterile container.

BABA GHANOUSH

This may well be my favourite way to eat aubergines, ever.

Highly recommend trying this out!

2 aubergines
1 clove of garlic
1/2 tsp chilli powder
1 tsp sumac
1 tsp smoked paprika
Juice and zest of one lemon
4 tbsp tahini
Coarse sea salt and cracked black
   pepper
Olive oil

1. Preheat your oven to 180°C / 350°F.
2. Cut the aubergines in half lengthways, score the flesh in a crisscross pattern, making sure you don't cut through the skins.
3. Drizzle with olive oil, then toss to coat.
4. Place on a baking tray flesh side up and bake for 35 minutes, or until soft.
5. Remove from the oven and scoop out the aubergine flesh from the skin.
6. Place all of the ingredients in your food processor and blend until smooth, adding some olive oil if needed. Serve and enjoy!

STICKY BBQ SAUCE

Brilliant on its own alongside any dish, this recipe really comes to life with my BBQ ribs recipe on page 149 – check it out!

30g grassfed butter
650g tomato passata
1 x 142g tin tomato purée
1/2 cup apple cider vinegar
1/3 cup blackstrap molasses
1/3 cup coconut aminos
4 cloves of garlic, minced
1 tsp chilli powder
1 tsp smoked paprika
Pinch of chipotle flakes
1/2 cup honey
Large pinch of coarse sea salt

1. In a large pot combine all of the ingredients.
2. Bring to the boil while whisking, then reduce to a simmer for 20 minutes.
3. Taste and ensure the seasoning is to your liking, remove from the heat and allow to cool before transferring to a sterile airtight container. (Keeps in your fridge for 1 week to 10 days.)

SWEET AND SAVOURY SNACKS

TOP COMBOS FOR ROASTED NUTS

I am nuts about nuts! Here's a selection of some of my top combos.

400g raw mixed nuts per recipe

Herby
2 tbsp coconut oil
2 tbsp Italian herb seasoning
Large pinch coarse sea salt

Chocolate
2 tbsp coconut oil
1 tbsp agave
2 tbsp cacao powder
2 tbsp rosemary
Large pinch coarse sea salt

Sweet and Spicy
1/4 cup honey
2 tbsp coconut oil
1 tsp chilli powder
2 tbsp coconut sugar
Large pinch coarse sea salt

1. Preheat your oven to 180°C / 350°F.
2. Place the nuts on a large baking tray and bake in the oven for 5 minutes.
3. In the meantime melt the coconut oil and mix with your chosen flavour combination.
4. Remove the nuts from the oven, coat in the flavour mix before placing back on the baking tray and baking in the oven for a further 10–12 minutes.
5. Allow to cool fully before storing in a sterile, airtight container.
6. Enjoy at your leisure!

ENERGY BALLS

Energy balls are the perfect snack for grabbing on the go; I always keep one in my handbag to beat the 3 p.m. slump. They are the perfect pick-me-up to see you right through to dinner.

'Not-ella' Balls
100g toasted hazelnuts, skin removed
2 tsp coconut oil
2 tbsp smooth nut butter of your
    choice
400g Medjool dates
100g oats
1 tsp vanilla extract
2 tbsp cacao powder
4–6 squares (100g) of your chosen
    dark chocolate, finely chopped
Good pinch of coarse sea salt

1. Add the nuts to your blender and pulse until they form a flour-like consistency, then add the oats and blend again for 2–3 minutes.
2. Next add the coconut oil, nut butter, dates, cacao powder and vanilla and pulse until combined.
3. Finally add in the chocolate and pulse lightly until combined.
4. Roll into balls and enjoy! I store mine in an airtight container in the fridge for up to a week.

The OG Wonky Balls
100g roasted cashew nuts
2 tsp coconut oil
2 tbsp cashew butter
400g Medjool dates
100g oats
1 tsp vanilla extract
Good pinch of coarse sea salt

1. Add the cashew nuts to your blender and pulse until they form a flour-like consistency.
2. Next add in the coconut oil, cashew butter, dates and vanilla and pulse until combined.
3. Finally add in the oats and the salt and pulse for a final time.
4. Roll into balls and enjoy! I store mine in an airtight container in the fridge for up to a week.

Nutfree Energy Balls
250g oats
150g dried cranberries
1 cup sunflower butter
1/2 cup maple syrup
1/2 tsp cinnamon
Good pinch of coarse sea salt

1. Mix all of the ingredients together in a large bowl.
2. Roll into balls and enjoy! I store mine in an airtight container in the fridge for up to a week.

ALMOND BUTTER CUPS

There is nothing I love more than when someone goes on holidays to the US and comes back with nut butter cups – I adore them and have absolutely no self-control, I HAVE to eat them all!

As a result, I've developed this slightly healthier version that can be stored in the freezer – allowing you take them out as and when you fancy.

Makes 8–10

For the chocolate:
10 tbsp agave
10 tbsp coconut oil
10 tbsp cacao powder
1/2 cup almond milk

For the centre:
1 tbsp almond butter per cup

Topping:
Large handful of flaked almonds
1 tbsp cacao nibs
Pinch of coarse sea salt

1. In a large pot combine the agave, coconut oil and cacao powder and heat over a low temperature until the coconut oil has melted.
2. Remove from the heat and whisk in the almond milk.
3. Line a cupcake tray with some cases, take half of the chocolate mixture and pour evenly into the bottom of each case.
4. Place a tablespoon of almond butter on top of the chocolate mixture in each case before pouring over the remaining chocolate.
5. Once the almond butter is covered, scatter with some flaked almonds, cacao nibs and coarse sea salt.
6. Place in your freezer to set for 1–2 hours, remove and allow to warm up to room temperature for about 15–20 minutes before serving. Enjoy!

SWEET POTATO CRISPS

I adore root vegetable crisps; there are some great brands out there doing really tasty, healthy ones but it's always nice to be able to do these types of things yourself.

450g sweet potato
1 tbsp garlic and chilli oil (see p. 195)
Large pinch of coarse sea salt

1. Using a mandolin, very carefully slice the sweet potato into thin slivers.
2. Preheat your oven to 200°C / 400°F.
3. Toss the sweet potato in the oil and lay out in a single layer on a large parchment-lined baking tray.
4. Sprinkle with a generous pinch of coarse sea salt before placing in the oven for 25 minutes.
5. Flip the crisps over after 10 minutes and allow to cook on the opposite side for the remaining 15.
6. Serve and enjoy!

BOUNTY BITES

Bounty bars – you either love them or you hate them. They're the marmite of the chocolate bar family. Personally, I love them and I love this healthier spin just as much as the real deal, if not more!

3 cups desiccated coconut
3/4 cup coconut oil, melted
4 tbsp maple syrup
1 tsp vanilla extract
250g dark chocolate

1. In your food processor blend together the desiccated coconut, coconut oil, maple syrup and vanilla extract for about 6–8 minutes until it forms a paste.
2. Press the mixture into a square silicone baking dish, ensuring it is evenly spread.
3. Melt the chocolate very gently and pour on top.
4. Place in your fridge to set for a couple of hours, until solid.
5. Portion into squares, serve and enjoy!

'NOT-ELLA' CRUMBLY COOKIES

Who doesn't love chocolate cookies? They're such a great little treat, especially with a cup of hot tea or coffee – not to mention reheated with some ice-cream.

Serves 8–10

1 cup almond or hazelnut butter
1 tsp vanilla
1 tsp coconut oil
2 tbsp cacao powder
2 tsp honey
1/2 cup coconut sugar
1 egg
Large pinch of coarse sea salt
50g dark chocolate, roughly chopped
   into chips

1. Preheat your oven to 180°C / 350°F.
2. In your mixer combine everything bar the chocolate.
3. Once the mixture is fully combined add in the chocolate and mix again.
4. Taking a tbsp of the mixture at a time, form into balls and place on a cookie sheet.
5. Gently press down on each ball to make into a cookie.
6. Bake in the oven for 12–15 minutes until cooked through.
7. Allow to cool on the cookie sheet before transferring to a wire rack.
8. Serve and enjoy.

ALMOND BUTTER FUDGE

When I was younger, I adored fudge. This version is so, so good; I constantly have a supply in my freezer for when my sweet tooth appears.

2 cups of almond butter
1/2 cup coconut oil
1/4 cup agave or maple syrup
Sprinkle of coarse sea salt
1 tbsp flaked almonds

1. In a small saucepan heat the almond butter, coconut oil and chosen sweetener for 4–5 minutes, whisking regularly until fully combined.
2. Line a cupcake tin with some paper cases and pour the mixture into them (depending on the size of your tin this recipe yields 6–8 large pieces of fudge).
3. Sprinkle some coarse sea salt and almond flakes on top before placing in the freezer overnight to set.
4. Remove from the freezer for a couple of minutes before serving and enjoy.

NUT BUTTER FLAVOURS X 3

There are endless possibilities when it comes to nut butter combinations.

The first task is to master a basic nut butter.

You will need: 300g raw nuts of your choice and a pinch of coarse sea salt

Cashew Coffee
1 cup cashew butter
1 tsp vanilla extract
1 tbsp instant coffee
1 tbsp maple syrup
Pinch of coarse sea salt

Chocolate Almond
1 cup almond butter
1 tsp vanilla extract
1 tsp coconut oil
2 tbsp cocoa powder
2 tsp honey
Pinch of coarse sea salt

Maple Cinnamon
1 cup of your chosen nut butter
2 tsp ground cinnamon
2 tbsp maple syrup
Pinch of coarse sea salt

1. Preheat your oven to 180°C / 350°F.
2. Place the nuts on a baking tray and put in the oven for 10 minutes until golden.
3. Once golden, remove and leave to cool to room temperature.
4. Once they have cooled, place the nuts in your food processor and blend for around 15 minutes, until a smooth mixture forms, adding in the salt at the end.
5. Once prepared, you can store in an airtight container for 1–2 weeks.

To make any of the flavour combinations, simply pop all of the ingredients into your blender and blitz for 2–3 minutes until combined. ☺

SWIRLY STRAWBERRY BROWNIES

A play on one of my very popular recipes that I hope you will love just as much!

Serves 10–12

3 eggs
1 1/2 cups almond butter
1 tsp vanilla extract
1/2 tsp baking powder
1/3 cup agave
1/4 cup cacao powder

Toppings:
2 tbsp almond butter (combined with
    a splash of water to loosen it out)
1/2 punnet of strawberries, hulled and
    halved
Small handful of flaked almonds

1. Preheat your oven to 180°C / 350°F.
2. Whisk all of the wet ingredients together until combined.
3. Add in the cacao powder and baking powder and whisk again.
4. Add the brownie mix to a baking dish (I find that silicone works best), then swirl in the extra almond butter, press in the strawberry halves and sprinkle over the flaked almonds.
5. Bake in the oven for 18–20 minutes until the brownies are nicely cooked.
6. Remove from the oven and allow to cool for 6–8 minutes before removing from the dish and slicing.
7. Serve and enjoy!

CRUNCHY CHICKPEAS

These are one of my favourite make-in-the-moment snacks. I can't get enough of them – perfect for any movie night!

Serves 4

400g tin of chickpeas, drained, dried and skinned
1 tsp piri-piri seasoning
1/2 tsp dried parsley
Good pinch of coarse sea salt

1. Preheat your oven to 180°C / 350°F.
2. Lay out the chickpeas on a baking tray in a single layer and bake in the oven for 40 minutes, tossing halfway through.
3. Once the chickpeas are ready sprinkle with the piri-piri, parsley and salt.
4. Sit back, relax and enjoy!

SWEET AND SAVOURY SNACKS

OIL-FREE POPCORN

I love popcorn, it's such a delicious snack – great if you're looking for something to tide you over until dinner time and don't want to fill up.

This is my standard go-to recipe; a little sprinkle of cayenne pepper works a treat too!

Serves 2

2/3 cup (140g) wholegrain corn kernels
Large pinch of coarse sea salt

    (30)

1. Place the kernels in a large pot with the lid on.
2. Place the pot over the heat and once you start to hear popping shake the saucepan continuously until it stops.
3. Remove from the heat and place the popcorn in a large bowl, toss in the salt and mix until evenly dispersed.
4. Hit the couch with a good movie and enjoy!

Sweet indulgence with a healthy twist. This section is dedicated to decadence, with three mouth-watering recipes for special occasions.

SHOWSTOPPER DESSERTS

PEAR AND ALMOND TART

Pear and almond tart is one of the first pastry dishes I ever learned how to make. Believe it or not, real deal pastry is something that I really enjoy making – it's one of the few traditional baking methods that I actually have the patience for. I had such fun coming up with this alternative recipe – it's so decadent and ready in half the time of a usual tart.

Serves 8–10

For the base:
250g ground almonds
3 tbsp coconut oil, melted
3 tbsp maple syrup
1 egg
Pinch of coarse sea salt

For the filling:
2 eggs
150g ground almonds
5 tbsp maple syrup
75g coconut oil, solid
1 tsp vanilla extract
1 tin of pears, drained and sliced

2 tbsp marmalade jam
Large handful of toasted almond
    flakes, to garnish

1. Preheat your oven to 180°C / 350°F.
2. Combine all of the base ingredients in a large bowl and mix well. It should be a crumbly mixture.
3. Grease an 8-inch pastry tin with a little coconut oil. Press the crust mixture tightly into the tin and up the sides.
4. Place some parchment over the pastry and fill with baking beans before placing in the oven to bake for 15 minutes.
5. While the base is cooking away, mix together all of the filling ingredients bar the pears.
6. Remove the base from the oven, store the baking beans carefully, remove the parchment paper, and pour the filling into the base.
7. Spread the filling evenly across the base and arrange the pear slices on top.
8. Bake in the oven for a further 15 minutes.
9. Remove from the oven, glaze with the jam and arrange the toasted almonds on top.
10. Once cooled remove from the tin, serve and enjoy!

CELEBRATION CAKE

A spin on a cake that I've had for every birthday since I was 3 years old! I hope it brings you many happy memories.

Serves 10–12

30g coconut oil
2 eggs
150ml honey
1 tsp vanilla extract
75ml almond milk
225g ground almonds
1 tsp baking powder
Pinch of coarse sea salt
20g smooth cashew butter
1/4 cup cacao powder

To decorate:
Large handful of toasted almonds
3 pots of chocolate-flavoured coconut
    yoghurt
3 chocolate buttons
1 glacé cherry

1. Preheat your oven to 180°C / 350°F and line an 8-inch round baking tray with parchment paper, then grease the edges with coconut oil to avoid any sticking.
2. Melt the coconut oil and add to a large mixing bowl with the eggs, honey, almond milk and vanilla extract; mix thoroughly until combined.
3. Next add the ground almonds, baking powder, cacao powder and salt, mixing thoroughly.
4. Lastly, add the cashew butter and mix until the mixture is fully combined.
5. Add the mixture to the baking tray and place in the oven for 35 minutes until golden and fully cooked.
6. Once the cake is fully cooked remove from the oven and allow to cool for 5 minutes before removing from the dish and placing on a wire rack to cool further.
7. Flip the cake every 10 minutes or so while cooling to avoid sticking to the rack.
8. Once fully cooled cut the cake vertically in half to make two semi-circles and sandwich them together with some of the coconut yogurt.
9. To form the nose, cut 2 diagonal slices from each side of the front of the cake and discard. Stand the flat edge on your serving place and cover the cake with the remaining coconut yogurt.
10. Smooth the yogurt over the nose and face, then create 'spikes' with the back of a spoon from the front to back over the rest of the 'hedgehog'.
11. Stick in the almonds at random to represent the prickles. Create the face with two of the chocolate buttons for eyes and the cherry for a nose, placing the final button at the back to create his tail. ☺
12. Serve and enjoy! (Best kept in the fridge.)

LIGHT AND DARK CHOCOLATE MOUSSE WITH RASPBERRIES

I adore this recipe. It is the ultimate indulgence for a special occasion.

Serves 12–14

White chocolate layer:
200g good quality white chocolate
300g coconut cream
2 tbsp agave
2 egg yolks
1 1/2 tsp gelatine and 2 tbsp water
1/2 tsp vanilla

Dark chocolate layer:
200g high percentage dark chocolate
2 tbsp coffee
320g coconut cream
3 tbsp agave
2 egg yolks
2 tsp gelatine and 2 tbsp water

1 punnet of fresh raspberries and
    some fresh mint leaves to serve

1. Line a loaf tin with some clingfilm, leaving plenty of overhang.
2. To make the white mousse, break up the chocolate and melt in a bowl over a bain-marie.
3. Add the coconut cream and stir until smooth before removing from the heat.
4. Place the gelatine and the water in a bowl and place over the bain-marie to dissolve.
5. Beat the eggs, agave and vanilla together before folding into the chocolate mixture.
6. Finally add the gelatine and pour into the tin and chill until set.
7. Once the white chocolate layer has set, move onto the dark chocolate layer.
8. To make the dark chocolate mousse, break up the chocolate and melt in a bowl over a bain-marie with the coffee.
9. Add the coconut cream and stir until smooth before removing from the heat.
10. Place the gelatine and the water in a bowl and place over the bain-marie to dissolve.
11. Beat the eggs and agave together before folding into the chocolate mixture.
12. Finally add the gelatine and pour into the tin on top of the white chocolate layer and chill until set.
13. Serve with fresh raspberries and a scattering of mint leaves. Enjoy!

GLOSSARY

GLOSSARY

Bain-marie – also known as a water bath (pot of simmering water with a bowl on top; the key here is to ensure that there is space between the bowl and the water).

Baste – to moisten food with melted fat or a highly flavoured sauce, usually during roasting, barbecuing or grilling.

Bind – to add egg, roux or melted fat to dry ingredients in order to combine them.

Blanch – to put food into cold unsalted water (or in the case of some vegetables, already boiling water), bring to the boil and simmer for a few minutes before draining.

Braise – to cook whole or large pieces of poultry, fish, meat or vegetables in a small amount of wine, stock or other liquid in a closed pot.

Butterfly – to slit a piece of food in half horizontally, cutting it almost all of the way through until it resembles a butterfly's wings. I particularly like to do this with whole chicken breasts in order to reduce the cooking time.

Caramelize – to cook sugar to the caramel stage. This is also used when grilling a sugar-based topping until brown or when glazing food in butter. At Christmas time I delight in caramelizing the top of our ham with some good quality maple syrup – it's out of this world.

Clarify – to clear a liquid of impurities; clarified butter is made by melting the butter and skimming it.

Confit – this comes from the French word *confire* (verb), meaning 'to preserve'. In the case of meat, such as duck, it is cooked in its own fat and covered so that it does not come into contact with the air. I really love nothing more than confit duck legs.

Coulis – A thin purée, usually of fresh or cooked fruit, which is soft enough to pour. (Something you might enjoy with my light and dark chocolate mousse on p. 233.)

Crudités – Raw vegetables, whether cut into slices or sticks, to nibble plain or with a dipping sauce. (Check out the sauces, dips and spreads section for some inspo!)

Deglaze – to dissolve congealed cooking juices or glaze on the bottom of a pan by adding liquid, scraping and stirring vigorously, while bringing the liquid to the boil. These juices can then be used to make gravy/added to a sauce.

Emulsion – a mixture of two liquids that are not mutually soluble, e.g. water and oil.

Fermentation – effervescence, usually caused by the action of enzymes.

Flake – to separate cooked food, particularly fish, so it falls into natural divisions. I adore flaking salmon into a salad!

Florentine – a dish made with or garnished with spinach – like eggs florentine, delish!

Frangipane – a sweet almond and egg filling that is cooked inside a pastry. (Check out my pear and almond tart on p. 229.)

Garnish – in classic cooking, garnish refers to one or more subsidiary ingredients appearing with one main ingredient in a dish. However, in layman's terms it's really just a sprinkle of something that you add at the end! For example, some fresh herbs. ☺

Glaze – a mixture that is brushed or sprinkled on the surface of food for colour or gloss.

Gratin – a dish cooked in the oven or under the grill so that it develops a brown crust.

Grease – to put fat (oil or butter) on a dish to prevent food from sticking to it.

Infuse – to immerse herbs, spices or other flavours into a hot liquid to flavour it.

Marinade – a mixture of oil, spices, or similar ingredients, in which meat, fish, or other food is soaked before cooking in order to flavour it.

Monte au beurre – a French term used to describe adding or whisking in whole, cold butter into a sauce or purée at the end of the cooking process.

Parboil – to boil or simmer until partially cooked.

Poach – to cook in liquid, usually water, just below simmering point so the liquid simmers in places rather than bubbling. A great one for eggs or indeed pears.

Provençale – a cooking style using olive oil, garlic, fresh herbs and sometimes tomato.

Refresh – to cool hot food quickly either by placing it under running water or plunging into iced water in order to stop it cooking. A great one to do with veggies to keep their crunch.

Sauté – to cook small pieces of food over a high heat, in fat, butter or oil, shaking the pan so that it 'jumps'.

Sear – to seal the surface of meat by cooking over a strong heat.

Score – to mark shallow or deep cuts in a decorative pattern with the point of a knife. This is particularly important when cooking whole fish so that it cooks evenly.

Shallow fry – cooking food in a small amount of fat or oil in a frying pan.

Sift – to shake a dry powdered substance through a sieve to remove any lumps/give lightness.

Simmer – to cook food gently in liquid that bubbles steadily just below boiling point so that it cooks in even heat without breaking up.

Sweat – to cook sliced or chopped food, usually veggies, in a little fat and no liquid over very low heat.

Zest – thin outer layer of citrus fruits containing the aromatic citrus oil, usually thinly pared with a vegetable peeler, grater or zester to separate it from the bitter white pith underneath.